# MODERN WORLD CULTURES

Africa South of the Sahara

◆

Australia and the Pacific

◆

East Asia

◆

Europe

◆

Latin America

◆

North Africa and the Middle East

◆

Northern America

◆

Russia and
the Former Soviet Republics

◆

South Asia

◆

Southeast Asia

◆

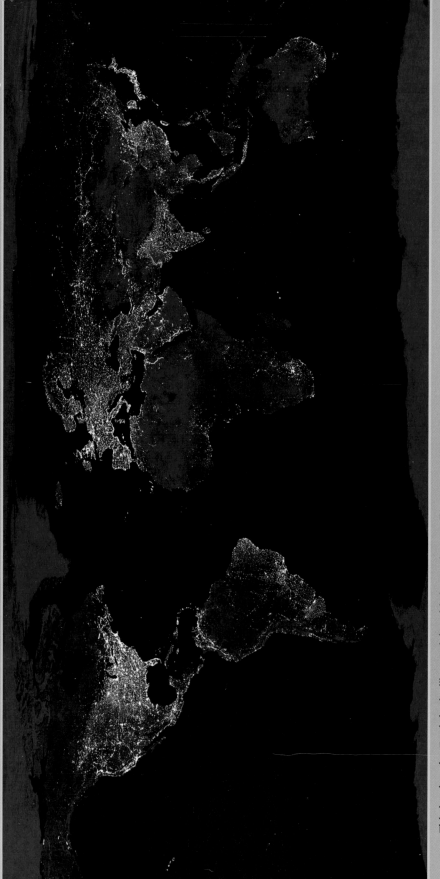

This is what the Earth looks like at night. This image is actually a composite of hundreds of pictures made by orbiting satellites. Man-made lights highlight the developed or populated areas of the Earth's surface. The dark areas include the central part of South America, Africa, Asia, and Australia.

(Credit: C. Mayhew and R. Simmon; NASA/GSFC, NOAA/NGDC, DMSP Digital Archive.)

MODERN WORLD CULTURES

# Africa
# South of
# the Sahara

Joseph R. Oppong

Associate Professor
University of North Texas

Series Consulting Editor
Charles F. Gritzner
South Dakota State University

CHELSEA HOUSE
PUBLISHERS

A Haights Cross Communications Company ®

Philadelphia

*Cover:* Women and children doing laundry in a stream in Axum, Ethiopia

CHELSEA HOUSE PUBLISHERS

VP, NEW PRODUCT DEVELOPMENT  Sally Cheney
DIRECTOR OF PRODUCTION  Kim Shinners
CREATIVE MANAGER  Takeshi Takahashi
MANUFACTURING MANAGER  Diann Grasse
PRODUCTION EDITOR  Noelle Nardone
PHOTO EDITOR  Sarah Bloom

Staff for AFRICA SOUTH OF THE SAHARA

EXECUTIVE EDITOR  Lee Marcott
EDITORIAL ASSISTANT  Joseph Gialanella
SERIES AND COVER DESIGNER  Takeshi Takahashi
LAYOUT  Maryland Composition Company, Inc.
DEVELOPMENTAL EDITOR  Carol Field
PROJECT MANAGER  Michael Henry

A Haights Cross Communications ↞ Company ®

www.chelseahouse.com

First Printing

10 9 8 7 6 5 4 3 2 1

Library of Congress Cataloging-in-Publication Data

Oppong, Joseph R.
  Africa South of the Sahara / Joseph Oppong.
    p. cm. — (Modern world cultures)
  Includes bibliographical references and index.
  ISBN 0-7910-8146-X (hard cover)
  1. Africa, Sub-Saharan—Juvenile literature. I. Title. II. Series.
  DT351.O66 2005
  967—dc22

                                        2005010039

# TABLE OF CONTENTS

Introduction                                      vi

1   Introducing the African World                  1

2   Physical Geography                            14

3   Historical Geography                          28

4   Population and Settlement                     41

5   Culture and Society                           55

6   Political History                             69

7   Making a Living                               81

8   Future of the African World                   98

    Appendix A                                   109
    History at a Glance                          110
    Further Reading                              114
    Index                                        115

# Charles F. Gritzner

Geography is the key that unlocks the door to the world's wonders. There are, of course, many ways of viewing the world and its diverse physical and human features. In this series—MODERN WORLD CULTURES—the emphasis is on people and their cultures. As you step through the geographic door into the ten world cultures covered in this series, you will come to better know, understand, and appreciate the world's mosaic of peoples and how they live. You will see how different peoples adapt to, use, and change their natural environments. And you will be amazed at the vast differences in thinking, doing, and living practiced around the world. The MODERN WORLD CULTURES series was developed in response to many requests from librarians and teachers throughout the United States and Canada.

As you begin your reading tour of the world's major cultures, it is important that you understand three terms that are used throughout the series: geography, culture, and region. These words and their meanings are often misunderstood. **Geography** is an age-old way of viewing the varied features of Earth's surface. In fact, it is the oldest of the existing sciences! People have *always* had a need to know about and understand their surroundings. In times past, a people's world was their immediate surroundings; today, our world is global in scope. Events occurring half a world away can and often do have an immediate impact on our lives. If we, either individually or as a nation of peoples, are to be successful in the global community, it is essential that we know and understand our neighbors, regardless of who they are or where they may live.

Geography and history are similar in many ways; both are methodologies—distinct ways of viewing things and events. Historians are concerned with time, or when events happened. Geographers, on the other hand, are concerned with space, or where things are located. In essence, geographers ask: "What is where, why there, and why care?" in regard to various physical and human features of Earth's surface.

**Culture** has many definitions. For this series and for most geographers and anthropologists, it refers to a people's *way of life*. This means the totality of everything we possess because we are human, such as our ideas, beliefs, and customs, including language, religious beliefs, and all knowledge. Tools and skills also are an important aspect of culture. Different cultures, after all, have different types of technology and levels of technological attainment that they can use in performing various tasks. Finally, culture includes social interactions—the ways different people interact with one another individually and as groups.

Finally, the idea of **region** is one geographers use to organize and analyze geographic information spatially. A region is an area that is set apart from others on the basis of one or more unifying elements. Language, religion, and major types of economic activity are traits that often are used by geographers to separate one region from another. Most geographers, for example, see a cultural division between Northern, or Anglo, America and Latin America. That "line" is usually drawn at the U.S.-Mexico boundary, although there is a broad area of transition and no actual cultural line exists.

The ten culture regions presented in this series have been selected on the basis of their individuality, or uniqueness. As you tour the world's culture realms, you will learn something of their natural environment, history, and way of living. You will also learn about their population and settlement, how they govern themselves, and how they make their living. Finally, you will take a peek into the future in the hope of identifying each region's challenges and prospects. Enjoy your trip!

Charles F. ("Fritz") Gritzner
Department of Geography
South Dakota State University
May 2005

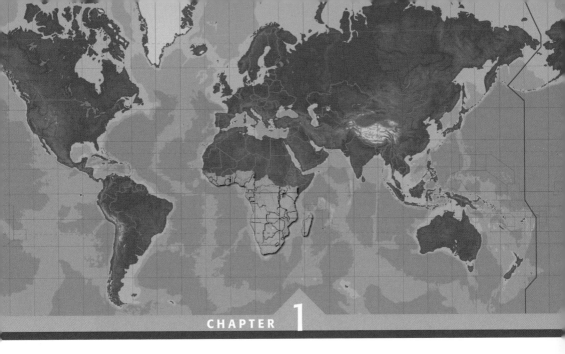

# CHAPTER 1

# Introducing the African World

Welcome to the African culture world, the birthplace of humanity! It is here, according to archaeologists, that culture first began, a development that marked the dawn of humankind. In the equatorial eastern part of the continent, our settlements, our tools and weapons, and our art began. Much later, the earliest humans gained control of fire and were able to make clothing and shelter that allowed them to leave their tropical homeland. More than one million years ago, they began to spread across the Old World to Asia and Europe. The cradle of humanity—what an incredible region to study!

For many people, the "African world"—the part of the continent that lies south of the Sahara Desert—is a place of emaciated children, AIDS, tragic civil war, grinding poverty, and hopeless despair. Less

Many African countries are rich in gold reserves. Ashanti Goldfields Company owns the Obuasi gold mine, one of Ghana's richest. To get the gold underground, the surface of the mountain has to be stripped. After extracting the gold, restoring the environment takes a very long time.

well known is the fact that the African world has some of the world's fastest-growing economies and the richest gold and diamond mines. According to the World Bank, from 1975 to 1995, the country with the highest annual economic growth worldwide was Botswana, an African country! In addition, Botswana's mines make it the world's biggest producer of diamonds. South Africa is the world's leading producer of gold. Yet, despite the massive gold, diamond, and oil deposits, many African people do live in abject poverty.

The African world is a region of amazing contrasts. The grandeur of physical landscapes reveals fascinating differences. In the east, majestic snow-capped mountain peaks tower above the deep Great Rift Valley. Vast stretches of savanna grasslands teeming with wildlife—the home of safaris—sharply contrast with dry, desert landscapes. In land area, Gambia, with an area of only 4,363 square miles (11,300 square kilometers), is tiny compared to gigantic Sudan, with 967,494 square miles (2,505,810 square kilometers), slightly more than one-quarter the size of the United States. Politically, the contrast is similar. Prosperous democratic governments such as Botswana and South Africa are neighbors to poor, repressive governments such as that of Zimbabwe.

As you can see, there is much to learn about the African world. The physical and cultural geography of the region is overwhelmingly rich and diverse. These themes are the primary focus of this book. In your journey through Africa south of the Sahara Desert, you will explore how people have culturally adapted to, used, and changed the various natural environments in which they live. You will learn how the amazing tapestry of African cultures differs from one location to another. The author, an African originally from Ghana, has attempted to provide a refreshing picture of the African world, including its many successes and promising future. Issues such as poverty, disease, and war, which are prevalent throughout much of the region, are also addressed.

Many titles can fit the African world. A few of them might be "geographic center of the world," "the abused world," "world of contrasts," and "home of world leaders." Africa is indeed the geographic center of the world. It is surrounded by other landmasses in all directions. Both the equator (0 degrees latitude) and the prime (or Greenwich) meridian (0 degrees longitude) pass through the continent. In fact, the African continent sits squarely astride the equator, with its northernmost and southernmost extremities lying at approximately 35 degrees latitude. This means that most of the African world lies within the tropical latitudes where weather is hot year-round and climates and seasons are distinguished only by differences in the amount and distribution of rainfall. It also means that disease-causing organisms such as mosquitoes and flies do not die off with a change in season. Instead, they are a general nuisance, often causing sickness, year-round.

The African world has been called an abused world. It suffered extreme devastation from slavery and colonial exploitation. Slavery alone took millions of its most productive people. During the era of colonialism, Great Britain, France, Germany, and Portugal cut Africa into pieces like a cake and devoured its natural resources as they built their empires. Many African countries still suffer from the lasting effects of this historical abuse and exploitation. In fact, the dividing of Africa is the underlying reason for many of Africa's continuing civil wars. As Europeans divided the continent, many traditional enemies were grouped together in the newly emerged "countries" and many families and tribal groups found themselves separated by political boundaries. Here is the story of Kofi from Ghana, West Africa.

Kofi is a member of the Akan-speaking people of West Africa and lives about 40 miles from Ghana's border with Côte d'Ivoire (Ivory Coast). Since childhood, Kofi has known that some of his family lives in Côte d'Ivoire and speaks French. In fact, when there is a funeral, many people from Côte d'Ivoire come to participate. Kofi looks forward to these visits because his uncles bring him nice gifts and his aunts spoil him. When he asked his mother why his relatives from Côte d'Ivoire have weird names and speak French, his mother explained that his aunts and uncles were descendants of his great-grandmother, Nana Aboagyewa. Some of Nana Aboagyewa's children lived in a village several miles away. When Great Britain and France divided West Africa, the boundary line divided the two groups of villages—the western part went to the French and the eastern part to the British. Ultimately, those in the French part went to French schools and adopted French culture in the modern country called Côte d'Ivoire and those in the eastern

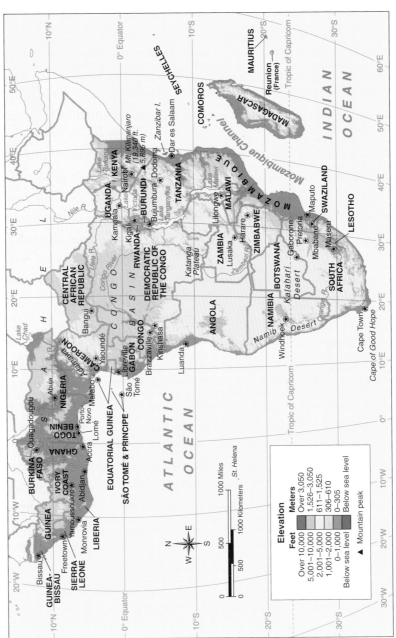

This reference map of Africa south of the Sahara shows the countries, cities, and major landforms of the region. A complete list of the countries in this region is given in Appendix A.

part, where Kofi lives, did not. They speak English and have been influenced heavily by British culture. Many years ago, when Kofi was about five, his uncle Assouan came from Côte d'Ivoire and took Kwesi, Kofi's older brother, to go and live with him. Kwesi now speaks French, is a national of Côte d'Ivoire, and has married and has children by an Ivorian wife.

The African world is a region of amazing contrasts. In Botswana, one in three of the urban adult population lives with HIV, but in portions of West Africa, very few people have the disease (less than 1 percent in Senegal). Fear of terrorism is high in Kenya, which has been bombed twice in four years by al Qaeda. In places like Ghana, peace and stable democracy promise a bright future. Corruption and religious riots are big problems in oil-rich Nigeria. South Africa, once divided by *apartheid* (a very strict form of racial segregation), now has a prosperous economy and is the leading destination of migrant workers—yet, the country has very high crime rates.

The African world is also the birthplace of many world leaders. Some of the world's best leaders, including Nelson Mandela, the former president of South Africa, and Kofi Annan, the current United Nations Secretary-General, were born in Africa.

## THE AFRICAN WORLD AS A CULTURE REGION

Before this book proceeds, Africa must be defined as a culture region. Geographers study where things are and try to understand how and why areas vary from one another. To identify areas that exhibit different characteristics, they use the concept of "regions," areas in which one or more identified features are similar. All features of Earth's surface can be classified by regions. This book examines climatic regions, landform regions, and regions rich in natural resources. It also focuses on economic, political, linguistic, and other cultural regional differences.

This book is one of ten in the series MODERN WORLD CUL-TURES. One feature that sets the African world apart from other regions is its unique cultural landscapes—the imprint of human activity on Earth's surface. Houses, villages, field patterns, and other visible human activities contribute to differences in the appearance of landscapes from place to place. Elements such as language, religion, art forms, and food patterns also are important components of culture. Quebec, the French-speaking region of eastern Canada has a different look and feel than the English-speaking region of western Canada. A French-speaking African from Cameroon will feel at home in Quebec in eastern Canada but completely lost in Alberta, another Canadian province, where most people speak English. Northern Sudan, where most people are Muslims and worship in mosques, is a distinct culture region from southern Sudan, where most people are Christians. This difference is one major reason for the long war between the two sides.

The concept of culture region is profoundly important. Cultural boundaries are arbitrarily drawn and are often marked by broad zones of transition. For this book, the boundary is drawn from the mouth of the Senegal River eastward to Lake Chad and continues in a southeasterly direction to a point north of the Jubba River in Somalia. To the north of this region is "North Africa," largely Arabic in culture and occupied by Arabic peoples who live in the desert and who, for centuries, followed a nomadic lifestyle. Defined in this way, the African world comprises 38 countries on the mainland and about 6.9 million square miles (17.9 million square kilometers) of land. (Please see Appendix A for a full listing of the countries, their land area, and their population.)

Most of the African world lies south of the Sahara Desert. Traditionally, the area has been occupied by black people who depended (and in many areas continue to depend) on subsistence agriculture, using very simple tools such as hoes and machetes. Hunting and gathering, animal rearing, and farming are the major occupations. Today, the region produces and exports many raw materials. Most of the region was "discovered" by Europeans during the sixteenth and seventeenth centuries and soon was heavily exploited under colonialism. European domination lingers throughout much of the region today. For example, Europeans drew the political boundaries between countries that today are a major cause of wars. They occupied parts of this region for more than a century and left only after vigorous struggle with the native Africans. Even today, the political and legal systems of most countries are based on European models.

## CULTURAL DIVERSITY, POVERTY, AND GOVERNMENT

The African world has remarkable cultural diversity. The primary indicator of cultural differences is language, and within the region more than 1,000 different languages are spoken. Many of these languages, however, have never been written and thus are unknown to the outside world. About 40 of these languages have more than one million speakers. In some countries, so many different local languages are spoken that people must adopt a *lingua franca* (a "borrowed" language spoken in common) in order to communicate with one another. Most countries use the colonial language—French, English, or Portuguese—as their official language for conducting government business. Today, as in the past, language is a major source of division and conflict in the African world.

Cultural practices in the region vary as widely as language does. Hundreds of ethnic groups—people united by similar culture, language, religion, customs, traditions, and racial ancestry who share a common sense of group identity—are the norm. In most countries, two or more major ethnic groups compete fiercely for political leadership. This sometimes produces conflict. An extreme example is the Hutu-Tutsi conflict in Rwanda that led to the massacre of more than 800,000 people in 100 days, perhaps the world's worst outbreak of genocide during the mid-1990s. In some countries, no major ethnic group emerges to provide leadership; instead, the numerous small ethnic groups fight among themselves to determine who will rule. This is the case in the Democratic Republic of the Congo, which has more than 200 distinct ethnic groups, most of which would like to lead the country.

Life and livelihood in the African world are very difficult. Extreme wealth and abject poverty often exist side-by-side. Because most people live on less than one dollar per day, Africans are jokingly called "magicians." Surely, anyone who can feed, clothe, and house a family of six on one dollar per day must be a magician. For many Africans, life is hard. According to the World Health Organization (WHO), a baby born in Sierra Leone in 2003 was more than 3 times as likely to die before its fifth birthday as a child born in India and more than 100 times more likely to die as a child born in Iceland or Singapore.

Subsistence farming is the most common occupation in Africa. Because many people depend on rain-fed agriculture, people who do not live in humid regions are always just one drought away from major famine or starvation. Ethiopia, one of the five poorest countries in the world, with an estimated income of just $100 per person per year, has experienced this repeatedly. In May 2003, an estimated 14 million Ethiopians faced starvation. Hospital wards were full of pitifully thin children, some of whom, like a five-year-old girl called Adanech, were too weak to hold down a few sips of milk. Every year, UN agencies and African governments estimate that millions of people face famine and starvation.

Despite their poverty, Africans spend astonishing amounts of money on lavish funerals, even when they are unable to feed the living. Funerals are a time for dressing up, drinking, dancing, and having fun. They can last up to seven days. In one case in Uganda, the son of a poor widow was forced to slaughter the

Funerals are a major celebration of the life of the dead, not only mourning the end of their life, and can be very expensive. They are a time for drinking, dancing, and providing a fitting "send-off" for the dead. At this funeral in Kumasi, Ghana's second-largest city, a professional musical group brought the music. Can you imagine how this can drive up the costs of funerals?

only milk cow he owned in order to prepare a meal for the mourners. The huge expense of funerals places a tremendous burden on families, driving many into long-term debt.

In the midst of all this, many multinational corporations are enjoying huge profits gained from Africa's natural resources. They exert almost colonial power–like influence as they exploit the region's oil, diamonds, gold, timber, and precious metals. In many ways, multinationals work hard to create an environment that allows extraction of the resource. Some influence domestic government policies through carefully targeted expenditures, bribes, and even military force. Most multinationals invest little or none of their profits in the local economy. By supporting one faction against another in fights for areas with rich natural resources, multinationals fuel civil wars to protect their interests. In such areas, instead of promoting economic progress and stability, the presence of resources actually aggravates instability. This situation has been called "the resource curse."

Political instability is widespread in the African world. Most countries have been independent for less than 50 years, and this short time has produced many brutal dictators including Idi Amin of Uganda, Mobutu Sese Seko of the Democratic Republic of the Congo, and Sani Abacha of Nigeria. Political corruption, embezzlement, and stealing public money for personal use are common. In many countries, military coups rather than elections mark political transitions. Many countries have experienced revolving-door military dictatorships, in which one military government kicks out another and rules until it is removed by yet another military government. Thankfully, this disruptive period of political history appears to be over and many promising democracies are emerging.

The African world is a region of religious tension and conflict. In 2002, at least 2,000 people died in clashes between Muslims and Christians in Kaduna, Nigeria. The longest religious conflict is in Sudan between the Muslim north and the mainly Christian and animist south. More than two decades of fighting has left 2 million people dead. The United States and the United Nations are leading serious efforts to bring peace. Perhaps the most realistic solution is to divide the country into two, a suggestion that is rejected by the more powerful north.

The African world is undoubtedly the world's finest and most famous safari destination. Zebras, hippos, giraffes, and elephants make places like Tanzania and Kenya favorite safari destinations for Americans and Europeans. Unfortunately, terrorism and rampant poaching threaten the huge potential of the emerging tourism industry.

## WHY DOES AFRICA MATTER?

Perhaps, after reading this far, you are wondering, "Why does Africa matter? Why should the United States be concerned about a remote region of the world that has so many problems?" Here are three good reasons.

First, recent developments in technology and travel have produced a world that is like a small neighborhood. Just as a fire in a neighborhood home concerns you, events in one part of the world easily affect other parts. Outbreaks of disease in one part of the world quickly spread to other parts if they are not controlled. This became clear during the outbreak of severe acute respiratory syndrome (SARS) in 2003. The disease started in South China and spread all over the world. When it was over, more than 8,000 cases and 812 deaths had been identified in 30 countries worldwide. In Canada, SARS killed 44 people, caused illness in hundreds more, and paralyzed the economy of Canada's richest province, Ontario, as hundreds of people were quarantined and countless others were bound with fear. Diseases do not need visas or passports to travel. They catch a free ride with people. Frequent global travel and trade binds the world together and puts everyone at risk. We need to know about what is happening in the African world and elsewhere in order to take measures that help ensure the safety of our homeland.

Second, since September 11, 2001, security is a major concern for Americans. On that day, terrorists hijacked and crashed three passenger aircraft into the World Trade Center in New York and the Pentagon in Washington, D.C. A total of 3,025 people were killed in the attacks. Osama bin Laden and the al Qaeda organization claimed responsibility for this wanton destruction of life and property. September 11 affected the global economy because people became afraid to fly. The United States has worked hard to prevent another terrorist attack. Protective measures included the creation of the Department of Homeland Security. September 11 also contributed to the U.S.-led military actions in Afghanistan and Iraq. Joint forces hope to ensure that these countries and others are unable to provide a safe haven for al Qaeda or similar organizations. Security for the United States and elsewhere demands that we know what is happening elsewhere in the world in order to take appropriate measures to prevent another attack. Osama bin Laden, for example, lived in Khartoum, Sudan, in the early 1990s, and he funded and trained terrorists in northern Sudan.

Third, we need natural resources such as oil from the African world. Continued conflict in the Middle East, the source of most of the world's oil, makes the oil supply uncertain. This means that we need to find new sources of oil. Thus, African oil-producing countries such as Nigeria, Gabon, and, recently, Sudan are of major interest to the United States. Peace and stability in the African world and friendship with the United States are keys to maintaining an adequate oil supply. For example, much of Sudan's oil lies in the south and existing fields straddle the north–south divide, an area of conflict. Consequently, an end to the war and a stable government in the Sudan are critical for the United States.

Let us begin our exploration of the incredibly beautiful, diverse, and troubled African world in earnest. Enjoy your safari to this land of warm climates and warm people. You may be rewarded by finding some gold or even diamonds. Watch out for viruses such as HIV/AIDS and Ebola, though. Let us think about how to control these viruses so that America will be safe. As we better understand the historical effects of slavery and colonialism, maybe we can help make Africa a better, more stable, and safer place. Let us try to find solutions to global problems such as poverty and terrorism as we visit the homeland of Kofi Annan, the United Nations Secretary-General. Let us explore humankind's motherland together. Welcome to the fascinating African world!

# CHAPTER 2

# Physical Geography

The African world is a land of incredible beauty and spectacular variety. Majestic snow-crested mountains lie adjacent to massive rift valleys. Dense rain forests, vast savanna and prairie grasslands teeming with wildlife, and massive parched deserts provide unparalleled variety. Africa does not have the world's highest peak, but it does have the longest river, the Nile, and the second-largest freshwater body, Lake Victoria. Africa has striking natural beauty, and its physical geography is surprisingly different from all the other continents.

## LAND FEATURES

Most continents have huge linear mountain ranges. South America has the Andes, North America has the Rockies, Europe has the Alps,

La Palm Beach Hotel in Ghana, a beautiful tropical tourist paradise. Such striking physical beauty may be observed throughout the African world. Few local residents can afford to stay at this 5-star luxury hotel.

and Asia has the Himalayas. The African continent does not have such mountain ranges. Instead, Africa is a huge plateau, resembling a raised platform, bordered by very narrow coastal lowlands. The highest point in Africa, Tanzania's volcanic Mount Kilimanjaro, is permanently covered in snow and glaciers. Other mountain ranges include the Atlas Mountains (in North Africa) and the Cape Range in the far south.

Instead of a north–south aligning mountain range, Africa has the unique north–south aligning Y-shaped Great Rift Valley. This feature is similar to the San Andreas Fault in California. Compared to the San Andreas Fault, which is only 780 miles (1,255 kilometers) in length, Africa's Great Rift Valley is enormous. Including the Red Sea extension, its total length is an incredible 6,000 miles (9,600 kilometers), making it Earth's longest fault. It has an average width of only 30 to 40 miles (48 to 64 kilometers). This long, deep depression flanked by steep wall-like highland cliffs is like a huge scar across Earth's surface. Along this scar, the land is patched with inactive volcanoes and a cluster of long, deep, narrow great lakes. Other than North America, Africa is the only continent that has a cluster of great lakes, and it is the only one with elongated great lakes that resulted from tectonic activity (movements of the Earth's plates). Lakes Tanganyika, Malawi, and Turkana are the largest of the Great Rift Valley lakes. Lake Victoria, Africa's largest, lies outside the Great Rift Valley.

Unlike other continents, Africa's coastlines are fairly smooth, with few indentations. Rugged coastlines provide excellent natural harbors. When these harbors are absent, as in most of Africa, humans have to construct harbors, usually at great expense. Moreover, sandbars block the entrances to most of the few good natural harbors. This prevents direct landing by large ocean vessels. These vessels usually dock far from the coast, and smaller surfboats haul the cargo to the shore. This increases the cost of shipping. In West Africa, the best natural harbors include Freetown in Sierra Leone and Banjul in Gambia.

The shallow part of the ocean that extends from the shore to the transition zone, where depth increases rapidly, is called the continental shelf. Such areas create an ideal habitat for fish and provide some of the richest fishing grounds in the world. Unfortunately, Africa's continental shelf is quite narrow and limited in extent, limiting potential for fishing and other activities such as offshore oil drilling.

## RIVERS

Africa has many great rivers. They drain the humid interior of the continent as they flow lazily and erratically along the plateau. The Nile River is the world's longest. Its waters flow 4,150 miles

(6,680 kilometers) as it passes from the humid equatorial high-lands, northward through a huge bend, and into the Mediterranean Sea through its famous delta in the desert of Egypt.

Like the Nile, Africa's many great rivers follow "erratic" courses. The mighty Congo River begins as the Lualaba River on the boundary between Zambia and the Democratic Republic of the Congo. For some distance, it flows northeast, and then it turns north and makes a U-turn. It heads in a southwesterly direction before finally cutting through the Crystal Mountains to reach the Atlantic Ocean. The Niger River originates from the Fouta Djallon Highlands, but instead of flowing directly into the ocean, for example through Sierra Leone, it heads off in a northeastern direction and then bends in a southeast direction before turning south toward the west African coast through Nigeria.

Because they cascade off Africa's interior plateau onto the narrow coastal plain, the continent's rivers provide some of the world's most scenic waterfalls and rapids. The most spectacular is Victoria Falls on the Zambezi River. As high and twice as wide as North America's Niagara Falls, Victoria Falls is a major tourist attraction. Unfortunately, such stunning waterfalls and rapids interrupt travel along Africa's major rivers. As a result, few rivers are navigable for any distance, and usefulness of the rivers for hauling goods is quite limited. The presence of rapids means that many rivers have great potential for hydroelectric power generation, however, although seasonal variations in river flow limit this potential. In fact, most African rivers vary seasonally in their flow. Peak flows occur during the rainy season, and some places experience flooding. During the dry season, flow declines drastically and many small rivers and streams dry up.

Seasonal variations in water levels also affect people and their lives. Farmers who depend on these rivers get poor yields. Sometimes, they can hardly feed themselves. When the water level is low, hydroelectricity production is also affected. Less

The Akosombo Dam on the Volta River is a major source of hydroelectric power for Ghana, Togo, Burkina Faso, and Benin. The lake formed behind the dam, Lake Volta, is the world's largest man-made lake.

electricity is produced, and this affects both industries and people. In fact, in some countries, power is rationed during the dry season. In many places, people have use of electricity for only 12 hours per day.

## CLIMATE AND VEGETATION

Geographers agree that climate is the single most important natural aspect of a region. It influences nearly all other elements of the physical environment, such as vegetation, animal life, water features, and soils, and it also is perhaps the major natural condition to which people must adapt.

### General Climate

The equator divides the African world into halves, north and south. This has two very interesting implications for climate. First, the climate patterns north and south of the equator are

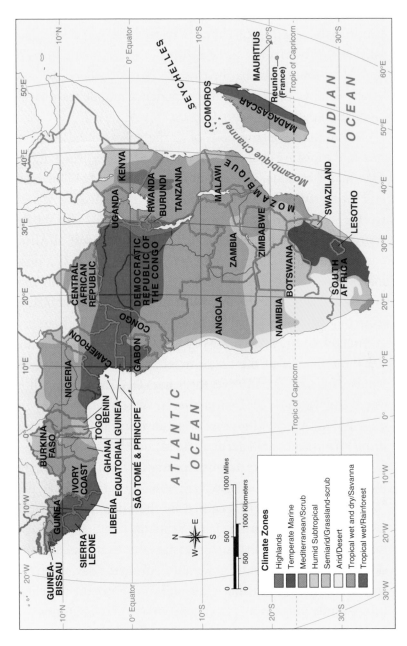

The equator bisects Africa, so that about two-thirds of the region lies within the low latitudes and has tropical climates. Africa has the most tropical climate of all the continents.

symmetrical—they are simply mirror images of each other. Second, because of Africa's equatorial location and symmetry, it receives abundant sunshine all year, resulting in most of the continent having tropical climates. Exceptions include the mid-latitude northern and southern tips of the continent, areas of high elevation, lands that lie close to coasts bordered by cold water currents, and regions that experience unique seasonal air circulation patterns.

An air mass is a large body of air that takes on the temperature and moisture characteristics of the area over which it lies. Two major air masses, the continental tropical (cT) air mass and the maritime tropical (mT) air mass, influence the African world. The zone where the two air masses meet is called the Intertropical Convergence Zone (ITCZ). In July, most of Africa comes under the influence of the mT air mass. Because it originates from over the Atlantic Ocean, this air mass is usually cool and saturated with moisture. Most of Africa gets its moisture from monsoon winds that are associated with this air mass.

In January, most parts of West and Central Africa come under the influence of the cT air mass and the northeast trade winds. This air originates over the Sahara Desert and brings hot, dry, dusty winds—called *harmattan* in West Africa—to the region. In East Africa, winds that originate over the Indian Ocean bring torrential rainfall particularly to coastal areas.

Generally, the more distant a location is from the ocean, the more extreme its temperature variations. Geographers call this "continentality," and it is caused by the differences between heating of land and water. Land heats more quickly but also loses heat more rapidly. In contrast, water heats much more slowly and loses heat more gradually. During the day, when the land is hot, the sea remains warm and moderates the temperature of lands adjacent to it through cool sea breezes. During the night, when the land loses its heat rapidly, the sea warms the land. Thus, the lowest temperature range occurs near the coast.

The highest occurs in the interior, far from the ocean or other large water bodies.

## Desert

There are two large deserts in Africa. The Sahara, in northern Africa, is the world's largest desert. This vast wasteland occupies nearly one-third of the continent. The Kalahari in southern Africa (a portion of which is called the Namib), is Africa's second desert. Desert temperatures can be scorching, regularly exceeding 100°F (38°C) and, by definition, deserts receive little moisture. The lack of soil moisture limits vegetation to places where water exists near the surface. Desert soils are low in organic matter but are not heavily leached of their nutrients; some are highly fertile and others heavily saline (salty) and very poor. The date palm is a commonly cultivated crop, and millet and sorghum are cultivated on a limited basis. Short-lived plants often sprout, bloom, wither, and die within a matter of weeks after periods of rare, but very precious, rains.

## Tropical Rain Forest

Tropical rain forests (incorrectly called "jungles") thrive in the humid tropics of the continent's equatorial region. Here, average temperatures are higher than 65°F (18°C) during even the coolest month of the year. Dense vegetation flourishes with the help of abundant rainfall every month, amounting to 60 or more inches (150 centimeters) annually.

Where rainfall is abundant, humidity tends to be high and insects, such as disease-spreading mosquitoes, abound. Malaria and yellow fever are just a few of the many illnesses that are common to African's rain forests. Malaria tops the list of diseases that threaten Africans. It kills up to one million children each year, and that figure has been increasing during recent years. Sleeping sickness, another devastating disease, is caused by the tsetse fly. It affects people and their livestock and has hindered the growth of livestock herds where meat could provide the protein needed to balance protein-deficient diets.

## Tropical Savanna

Sandwiched between the equatorial rain forests and the more poleward-located deserts is the tropical savanna—perhaps Africa's best-known ecosystem. Here, tall grasslands and scattered trees create Africa's famous savannas, home to the continent's huge herds of big game animals. This unique environment is created by a pattern of seasonal rainfall. During low sun season (winter), atmospheric controls and conditions similar to those of the adjacent deserts bring drought to the region. During the high sun season (summer), however, controls that influence conditions year-round in the humid tropics spread over the area, bringing 40 to 80 inches (100 to 200 centimeters) of often drenching rainfall. The savanna region is home to most of Africa's national parks and game reserves, including the famous Serengeti National Park. The Serengeti, which means "extended place" in the Masai language, has the largest gathering of big game in Africa. Millions of grazing wildebeest, zebras, gazelles, giraffes, elephants, and buffalo roam the land in huge herds; they are preyed on by their fierce natural enemies: lions, leopards, and hyenas. This is safari country.

Ecotourism—travel to natural areas to understand the physical and cultural qualities of the region—has become an important industry in Africa's savanna country. The economies of Kenya, Tanzania, Uganda, and Mozambique, in particular, receive a huge boost from visitors. Today, most safari hunting is done with a camera rather than a gun. Nonetheless, illegal poaching is ravaging wildlife populations in many locations and threatens the ecotourism industry.

## Steppe

Immediately poleward from the savanna regions are areas of semiarid steppe. Here, rainfall is transitional between the savanna and desert regions, or about 10 to 20 inches (25 to 50 centimeters) each year, with much higher annual variation. Prolonged droughts are quite common in this region, which transitions into the true desert. Temperatures often soar over 100°F (38°C). Grazing of livestock is the primary human activity in this region.

## Highlands

Highland regions are located in isolated mountainous areas of southern and eastern Africa. The temperature, amount of rainfall, and soil conditions vary according to elevation and other environmental conditions. In Ethiopia, much of which lies more than 8,000 feet (2,438 meters) above sea level, the daily temperature falls to 55°F (12.8°C) in January. Frost often occurs in the mountains of Tanzania. Although Mount Kenya sits right across the equator, its peak is capped with snow. Africa's highest mountain, the majestic 19,340-foot (5,895-meter) Mount Kilimanjaro, also has a snow-capped peak.

Thick mountain forests develop in the highlands, where abundant precipitation, moderate temperatures, and deep and fertile soils combine to promote dense tree growth. Most of Africa's highland regions have fertile soils that have been farmed intensively for many years.

## ENVIRONMENTAL PROBLEMS

Africa faces many serious environmental problems. It is important to remember that Earth is humankind's "life-support system." When resources become limited or the environment is polluted, humans suffer.

## Dwindling Forests

The continent's forests are disappearing rapidly as logging, farming, and overuse result from rapid population growth. When the forest cover is removed, water runs off slopes more rapidly and soil erosion increases. Soil erosion threatens food

These beautiful palm trees are part of the Aburi Botanical Garden. The African world boasts many beautiful national parks and botanical gardens. In East Africa, many parks are wildlife preserves. Unfortunately, urban development is encroaching on such parks and conservation land uses.

production and livelihood. Because forests are "scrubbers" of Earth's atmosphere, even the global climate may be affected by deforestation.

### Declining Wildlife

In rural areas, many people still depend on hunting wildlife. Let us follow Yaovi and Victor, two 20-year-old men as they go hunting in Togo, West Africa, during the dry season. Two dogs accompany them. They don't have guns; they have machetes (long knives). As they come to a patch of dry grassland, they set fire to it and wait. Soon, the fire is a raging inferno. Instead of running for their lives, they wait excitedly. First, a deer emerges, fleeing the fire. The two dogs run after it. The deer runs, faster, faster, faster, but soon, it is out of breath and collapses. Victor is there and kills it with his machete. After about four hours, they have quite a haul—they have taken two antelopes and several smaller animals. They take their haul home, sell some, and enjoy a feast of "bushmeat" while the fire burns on. Next week, they will probably go hunting again.

The activities of hunters such as Yaovi and Victor and of poachers (illegal hunters) have destroyed much of Africa's wildlife. In Africa's savanna, poachers target big game such as elephants and rhinos. The black rhino suffered a near-catastrophic decline from about 65,000 animals in the 1970s to only 2,400 in the mid-1990s. Illegal demand for horn, high unemployment, poverty, demand for land, and wars all contribute to the declining populations. Rhino horn is highly sought after by practitioners of traditional medicine in China. In the Middle East, it has traditionally been carved and polished to make dagger handles. Similarly, poachers kill elephants for their valuable ivory trunks.

### Threat of Climate Change

Some scientists believe that the world's climate is changing. They suggest that Earth is getting warmer and that such warming will

Fisherman bring their catch to the Elmina Fish Market. Fish is a major source of protein in coastal regions, but dwindling fish stocks due to overfishing is a major concern.

change the world as we know it. In Africa, the threat of global warming is a major concern. Increased drought and evaporation will dramatically affect household food security. In the extreme, this could lead to social disruptions and displacement of people because of drought. Also, global warming could extend the area at risk for malaria southward and northward into the Mediterranean climate region. Thus, a host of problems, including an increase in malaria and other tropical diseases, diarrhea, malnutrition, and acute respiratory infections, are forecast for the African world.

In addition, reduction in fish stock size and distribution can be expected in Africa's limited marine ecosystem, such as that in Namibia. The effect of such changes on the established fisheries is likely to be disastrous. Africa's seas and oceans are already threatened by wastewater, airborne pollution, industrial effluent (pollutant waste), and silt from inadequately managed watersheds.

Climate changes aside, many African countries are facing absolute water shortage. In Namibia, which is ranked among countries that are most likely to be affected by climate change, water resources will be the hardest hit. The greatest impact is likely to be in the interior locations with limited rainfall.

## Weather and Food Security in Southern Africa

Historically, late and erratic rains followed by floods have jeopardized crops and food supplies in southern Africa. Although crop prospects improve with increased rainfall, intense rains in parts of Zambia and Angola recently caused many rivers to overflow. Widespread flooding with disastrous consequences occurred in western Zambia and parts of Angola, Namibia, Botswana, and Zimbabwe. The heavy rains damaged the crops so much that emergency food relief became necessary. Madagascar was hit by cyclones (storms similar to hurricanes) in 2004, causing large-scale damage, destroying crops, and directly affecting 774,000 people.

Floods destroy crops in some areas, but in others, drought is the major problem. During recent years, unusually dry weather conditions drastically decreased the harvest prospects in Zimbabwe, South Africa, Lesotho, Swaziland, and parts of Malawi and Angola. Zimbabwe, in particular, has faced a potentially critical food shortage that affected more than 2 million people in 2004.

Having reviewed some of Africa's environmental problems, let's turn our attention to its equally fascinating culture history. We will try to understand how Africa's historical past explains the present problems and examine the future prospects.

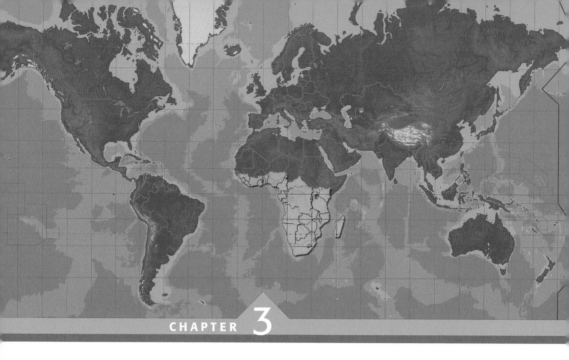

# CHAPTER 3

# Historical Geography

Most archaeologists (scientists who study early humans) believe that Africa was the birthplace of humankind and that from here humans eventually migrated to other parts of the world. Culture—including language, tools, weapons, and the use of fire—began in Africa. All available archaeological evidence suggests that humans can trace their ancient ancestral roots to the African continent.

Whereas much is known about the earliest humans from the archaeological record, we know very little about their "documented" history until about 500 years ago. Most of the region lacked writing, and thus a written history, until the sixteenth century. Without written records, establishing the exact details of life and livelihood in the African world before the modern era is difficult. Today, cultural and

historical geographers, anthropologists, and historians are trying to piece together this early history from folklore, poetry, art,
and similar sources.

From what is known, our early ancestors were truly fascinating. Rock paintings show that they survived by hunting and
gathering and used stones for tools and weapons. Much later,
perhaps 5,000 years ago, some people began to raise sheep and
goats. These early peoples were able to meet the challenge of different and often extreme physical environments. In northeastern Nigeria, they established terraces on hillsides for farming. In
Kenya, they dug irrigation canals and constructed stone-lined
wells. To the south, in Zimbabwe, they built massive stone-
walled structures without the use of cement. Perhaps 2,500 years
old, these walls still stand today. The Great Zimbabwe Ruins, as
this historic site is called, and other archaeological evidence, re-
veal cultures with highly advanced technologies.

## EARLY CULTURE HEARTHS

A culture hearth is a source region of a particular culture or
people sharing a common way of life. From here, new ideas or
cultural practices diffuse, or spread to new areas. Cultural diffusion occurs in two main ways. First, people learn from each
other as they observe their friends and neighbors. Soon, the area
of practice expands to cover a much larger area. Second, as people move to new places, they take their culture with them to the
new place; they begin to build homes and establish farms just
the way they did back home. Arab traders brought the Islamic
religion and culture into the northern parts of West Africa. At
first, it was mainly a religion of the rulers: The king of ancient
Ghana and his court converted to Islam in the twelfth century.
From there Islam, spread to other parts of West and East Africa
and northern Sudan. Generally, beginning in Southern Africa,
the farther north you go, the more Muslim it becomes.

Four main culture hearths have been identified in the African
world: the Ethiopian Plateau, the West African savanna, the West

African forest, and the forest savanna boundary. Perhaps the best known hearth is the Kush kingdom which, with its capital Meroë, flourished around 2000 B.C. Stone walls, palace buildings, and temples confirm the existence of a well-organized people with stone and iron technology and social, political, and religious order. Crops, agriculture methods, textiles, pottery works, basket weaving, and irrigation techniques diffused from Kush to adjacent areas and, ultimately, to distant lands.

Other ancient culture hearths that developed iron technologies include the Nok culture in central Nigeria and Axum in Ethiopia. Their legacy of clay figurines (both animals and humans) suggests that the Nok had extensive experience with stone and iron tools. The Axum culture showed remarkable engineering, architecture skills, and metal processing. In West Africa, the ancient empires of Ghana, Mali, and Songhai flourished with gold mining, pottery, textiles, and trade.

Many plants were domesticated and cultivated in the African world. They include millet and sorghum, yams, oil palm, castor oil, okra, watermelons, coffee, and cotton. That is a long list. Next time you eat a slice of watermelon or wear a cotton garment, you can thank Africa!

## TRADE IN ANCIENT WEST AFRICA

Remember the last time you traded your sandwich for a friend's candy bar? You had something you did not want or need and found somebody who wanted it. Your friend had something that you wanted and was willing to trade. That is the concept of complementarity. The northern part of West Africa is very dry compared to the southern part. As a result, the goods produced in the two areas tend to be complementary. Forest people in the south produced ivory, spices, and dried food, all of which were needed in the north. The northern peoples produced salt, which people in the south lacked. People in the middle profited from the trade between the north and the south. Thriving centers of commerce emerged in these middle areas: Timbuktu, in modern Mali, and Kano, in Nigeria, grew to be prosperous ancient urban centers because of this trade.

## EUROPEAN CONTACT WITH THE AFRICAN WORLD

The first meaningful European contact with the African world was in the fifteenth century, when Portuguese explorers sought a sea route to India. When they found plentiful ivory and gold along the West African coast, they named the areas accordingly—Ivory Coast and Gold Coast. They set up several trading posts and exchanged copper and brass products for African gold. Seeing the Portuguese success, the other European powers—the French, Spanish, Dutch and British—joined the fray. Trade in complementary goods continued until about 1492, when the Americas were discovered.

### The Silent Trade

How do people trade when they don't speak the same language? Have you been wondering how the Europeans and Africans agreed on an appropriate and fair exchange or price? At this time, Africans and Europeans did not have a common, universally accepted currency. In parts of West Africa, cowrie shells (a type of seashell) were used as currency. For trade with foreigners, however, the barter method of exchange was used. Barter is very similar to what happened with your sandwich trade, but with one major difference: Because of differences in language, negotiating an acceptable exchange was not possible. Traders conducted business without language. This was called the silent trade. Let us watch as Kofi Antobam, a farmer in coastal Ghana, buys a gun from Diego, the Portuguese merchant.

After displaying his wares in the open clearing, Diego withdraws to watch from a distance. Kofi Antobam approaches cautiously, examines the gun, and smiles with satisfaction. He leaves some gold beside the gun and withdraws to watch from a distance. Diego approaches, considers the offer, and, if he is dissatisfied, shakes his head and leaves both the gold and the gun. Kofi Antobam returns and adds a little more gold (increases his bid) and withdraws. This cycle continues until they reach an acceptable exchange. When that happens, Diego takes the gold, smiles with satisfaction, and leaves the gun. Kofi Antobam then takes the gun and goes his way. If Kofi Antobam thinks that Diego is asking too much, he simply takes his gold and leaves the gun.

## The Slave Trade

Beginning in the seventh century, slaves were a major export from the African world. Three main phases can be identified: the trans-Saharan slave trade, East African slave trade, and the transatlantic slave trade.

When camels were introduced into northern Africa during the seventh century, trade between North Africa and Africa south of the Sahara increased greatly. The dry desert north needed products from the southern forest and savanna peoples. Armaments, books, textiles, and beads were exported from the northern Islamic states. In return, the African world sold gold, ivory, and slaves. This trade was conducted along a small number of trade routes. An estimated 9.4 million slaves were sent this way. The majority were women who would become concubines or house servants in North Africa and Turkey. Male slaves usually served as soldiers. Because of the long journey across the desert by foot, many of the slaves, if not most, died before reaching their destination.

About 5 million slaves were also sent from East Africa to Asia, including Persia (Iran), India, and China. This was called the East African slave trade. These slaves were primarily women and children who became concubines and household servants.

The transatlantic slave trade had the most vicious and widespread impact. After European diseases had decimated the indigenous populations of America, the European settlers identified African slaves as an ideal source of labor for their plantations and mines. For this trade in human resources, the

The Elmina Slave Castle, established by the Portuguese, was a major shipping port for slaves destined for the Americas. Today, it is a museum and a major tourist attraction.

Europeans built castles along the West African coast, particularly in Ghana. Many of these castles still stand and today are a major tourist attraction.

The slave trade was an important element of the "triangular trade," as the transatlantic trade was called. European ships carried guns, alcohol, and manufactured goods from Europe to West Africa. These goods were exchanged for slaves. The slaves were transported to the Americas, where they were exchanged for gold, silver, tobacco, sugar, rum, and other products required in Europe.

The slave trade was a disaster for Africa. An estimated 10 million slaves (the actual number will never be known) were sent to the Americas. This is not the worst part. For every one slave that arrived in the Americas, several more died either during slave raids and wars that resulted from them or in transit across the Atlantic Ocean. To avoid being captured and sold, African farmers tried to hide and could no longer go to their farms. This disrupted agriculture and produced widespread famine, chaos, and disease that killed many more. We can only wonder what Africa would be like today had these millions of healthy, young people, in the most productive part of their lives, not been removed.

In the Americas, slave labor contributed toward the building of what was to become the world's strongest economy through their work on the plantations and in mines. Even after the abolition of slavery, former slaves contributed to the economy as sharecroppers, laborers, and skilled workers. We can only wonder what America would be like today had there been no slavery.

## DIVIDING AFRICA

Slavery was abolished in Great Britain in 1807 and throughout the British Empire in 1833. Europeans then turned their attention to real trade, exploration, and occupation of the interior of the African continent. Two key reasons were to spread Christianity and to find new areas for profitable trade. Initially, the Europeans established small trading posts along the coast, some of which used the former slave castles. Each group tried to expand its trade area in order to avoid competition and increase profits.

Soon, the Europeans began to fight among themselves. The French, for example, were angry when the British annexed Egypt to guarantee them unlimited access to the Suez Canal. To cut them off, the French pushed forward from their coastal bases toward Lake Chad, northward from Côte d'Ivoire and Benin and southward from Algeria. They also annexed Madagascar. In short, the major European powers were competing to secure the most productive and heavily populated areas.

To avoid further fighting and competition among themselves, the European powers held a conference at which they divided the African continent among themselves. In what came to be known as the Berlin Conference of 1884–1885, without any consideration of or input from the African natives, African lands were parceled and traded as American children might trade baseball cards.

The process of drawing political borders for the convenience of European powers created major cultural chaos. In many places, people united by language or religion were ripped apart by political boundaries. Elsewhere, traditionally hostile societies were thrown together. In West Africa, the Ewe-speaking people were divided by the political boundary. Half of them were in the Gold Coast and ruled by the British, and the French controlled the other half. The Hausa-Fulani people were split between Nigeria (British rule) and Niger (French rule).

## COLONIAL RULE

European colonial rule involved imposing European ways on Africans. Africans were forced to adopt European language, religion, political systems, and other cultural practices. European education taught Africans to be ashamed of their culture. Native African religions were seen as paganism or witchcraft and were often banned. A primary goal of European occupation was to "civilize" these primitive Africans.

European rule in Africa had one common purpose: the exploitation of Africa's people and resources. The system of rule varied significantly among the different groups. Democratic governments ruled in Britain and France, but dictators ruled Spain and Portugal. The colonial government policies seemed to reflect these differences.

The British adopted indirect rule. African rulers were taken over and required to function as representatives of Britain. The chiefs collected taxes, enforced colonial laws, and performed other duties assigned by the colonial authorities. In exchange for this service, they received protection from their enemies and occasional gifts. In this way, the British ruled indirectly and did not have to deal directly with Africans.

The French approach was assimilation. Africans were pressured to adopt French culture, including language, religion, and customs. In fact, if they became French enough, these Africans could vote in French national elections.

In the Portuguese and Belgian colonies, harsh, direct exploitation was the norm. In the Belgian Congo, the entire population was forced to gather rubber, kill elephants for their ivory, and build roads for export routes. Those who did not meet their quotas, sometimes entire communities, were massacred. This cruel and harsh exploitation killed about 10 million Congolese, half of the entire population, by the end of King Leopold's reign of terror. Little was invested in these natives. At the time of independence, the area occupied by the entire modern Democratic Republic of the Congo had only 16 university graduates.

## THE IMPACT OF COLONIALISM

Much of the current political instability in Africa can be traced to the dividing of the continent by European powers nearly 150 years ago. Geographers identify nations and states as divisions. A nation is the territory occupied by a nationality of people. Such groups are generally united by language, religion, and other cultural practices. States are sovereign political entities. When a political entity comprises more than one nation, it is called a "multination state." Most African countries today are multination states. Sometimes, one nation is divided among multiple states. When this happens, it is called a "multistate nation." Very few African world countries are nation–states, in which one nationality of people also is self-governing within its own political territory.

Multination states are notorious for political instability. Competition among the different nations for political control is

Elementary school children play during recess in Asankrangwa, Ghana. Unlike urban schools, rural schools such as this one are poorly equipped. Frequently, basic educational materials such as paper and pencils are not available. Despite this, the children have a good time playing with each other.

a constant source of strife and discontent. In Nigeria, for example, the major nations include the Ibo in the southeast, the Yoruba in the southwest, and Hausa and Fulani in the north. The struggle among these nations for political domination is one reason for Nigeria's history of military coups and instability.

Multistate nations are also areas of political strife. Resenting the separation, such culture groups usually want to separate and join their relatives. The Somali people have always dreamed about uniting in one great state called Greater Somaliland. To fulfill this dream would mean breaking away Somali-dominated parts of Kenya and Ethiopia and giving those to Somalia. That will probably never happen peacefully.

Colonialism provided a basic infrastructure of roads and railways that continues to be used today. Unfortunately, linking rail services together has been extremely difficult. During the colonial era, each country had its own track gauge (width), as well as its own braking and coupling systems. This made it impossible for trains to pass from one country to another.

Schools and modern health care were also introduced during the colonial era, but colonial education and Christianity presented everything European as "superior" and everything African as "inferior." African healing methods were branded as "witchcraft" and banned or severely discouraged. As a result, some educated Africans rejected and felt ashamed of their heritage.

Moreover, because Africans were forced to produce agricultural goods for European industry, traditional food crops were neglected. This laid the foundation for the current situation in which many African countries must import basic foods. As Ali Mazrui, renowned African scholar, stated, Africans produce what they do not eat, and eat what they do not produce.

## THE STRUGGLE FOR INDEPENDENCE

Because of decades of exploitation and suffering, Africans began to fight for independence and self-rule. Educated Africans studying in the United States and Europe began the fight by declaring that "Africa is for Africans." In a series of meetings held between 1900 and 1946, they wrestled and argued for independence. After their education, some of these African intellectuals, such as Kwame Nkrumah of Ghana and Nnamdi Azikiwe of Nigeria, returned home and established political parties and newspapers to continue the fight for self-rule. Similarly, Africans who had fought in European battles such as World Wars I and II came back and began to organize their people to fight for self-rule.

When Kwame Nkrumah returned to Ghana from the United States in 1947, he established the Convention People's Party (CPP) to press for "self-government now." In 1948, police brutality against a peaceful demonstration by former soldiers to express their grievances turned into a massive riot. The colonial government blamed, arrested, and imprisoned Nkrumah and other political leaders. This seemed to only increase their determination and resolve. When he called for a nationwide strike to demand independence, he was imprisoned again—but he emerged as a national hero. While in prison, his party won a landslide victory in municipal elections. Nkrumah could no longer be stopped. The British quickly granted internal government, and, on March 6, 1957, independence finally arrived in Ghana. In his independence speech, Nkrumah noted amidst the celebrations, "At long last the battle has ended. And our country, Ghana, is free forever! . . . We again rededicate ourselves in the struggle to emancipate other countries in Africa, for the independence of Ghana is meaningless, unless it is linked up with the total liberation of the African continent."

In other parts of the African world, the battle was far from ending. In fact, it had just begun. Kwame Nkrumah worked with leaders from these countries to secure independence in the rest of Africa. He held various conferences to mobilize the people towards African independence and unity. In 1958, at the All-African People's Congress held in Accra, Ghana, Nkrumah gave a stirring challenge:

> I appeal to you in the sacred name of mother Africa to leave this conference resolved to rededicate yourselves to the task of forming among the political parties in your respective countries, a broad united front, based upon one common fundamental aim and object—the speedy liberation of your territories. This decade is the decade of African independence. Forward then, to independence, to independence now! Tomorrow, the independent States of Africa.

Similar struggles for independence continued in other places. In Kenya, for example, where the best land had been reserved for white settlers, the native Kikuyu formed the Kikuyu Central Association to demand independence and take back the stolen land. During the World Wars, they had seen *mzungu* (whites) terrified, wounded, and killed. The invincibility of mzungu was broken forever. These energized, returning soldiers urged Kenyans to fight for their rights, and led in the Mau Mau conflicts. When it was over, about 11,000 Kenyans had been killed, but, the scale of effort needed to put down the Mau Mau and other uprisings had convinced mzungu that it was time for a change. Kenya became independent under Jomo Kenyatta in 1963.

Many African countries achieved independence in 1960, and by 1965, most had attained independence. In areas where the colonialists had settled permanently, such as Angola and Mozambique, however, independence came only after civil war. Similarly, in Zimbabwe, the British had to be forced out. Robert Mugabe emerged as president after an eight-year civil war with the white minority government that ended in 1980.

Hard-won independence tasted sweet, but for many African countries, it quickly turned sour. The seeds of discord, sown by the imposed political boundaries under colonialism and growing economic difficulties, proved too difficult to handle. For many countries, with independence came poverty, corruption, and political chaos, rather than freedom and prosperity.

# CHAPTER 4

# Population and Settlement

In 2004, about 584 million people lived in the African world. The population is growing at 2.5 percent per year and is expected to double in about 27 years. About 46 percent of the population is younger than 15 years of age. Africa's population distribution is not uniform. Population density measures the average number of people per unit area of land. This varies significantly among and within countries. The most densely populated areas tend to be near rivers, lakes, and oceans. In contrast, desert and savanna areas tend to have very sparse population. Overall population density is about 74 people per square mile (27 per square kilometer). Rwanda and Burundi have the region's highest population densities.

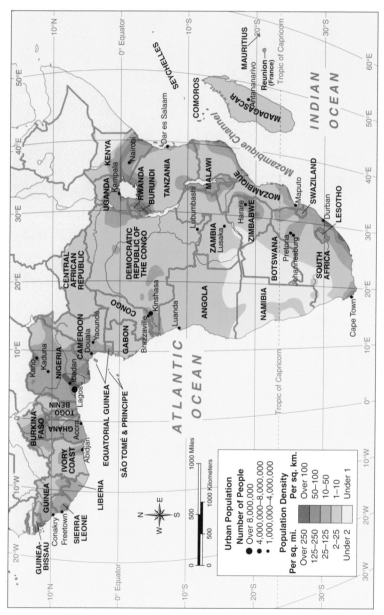

Africa south of the Sahara has an average population density that is less than that of the United States. The majority of the region's people live in a few small, densely populated areas. While there are some areas with a high population density, much of the region is sparsely populated.

Three major areas of population concentration can be identified. First is the coastal area that stretches from Dakar in Senegal, through Côte d'Ivoire, Ghana, and Nigeria, and to Libreville in Gabon. A second major concentration stretches from the Ethiopian Highlands to Lake Victoria. Finally, the copper belt, which covers the Democratic Republic of the Congo and Zambia, is another major area of high population concentration.

By far, the most populous country in the African world is Nigeria, with 129 million people and a rapidly growing population. In 1950, it had a population of about 33 million, but at current rates of increase, it is expected to explode to almost 339 million by 2050. If this occurs, there would be no historical precedent—a tenfold population increase within one century!

The least densely populated areas tend to be desert regions. Zones of sparsely populated regions include the Sahel region, which extends from Dakar to Mogadishu. Mali and Central African Republic have particularly low densities because drought is a persistent problem. A second area of sparse population is the forest region of west-central Africa, which includes Gabon and the Democratic Republic of the Congo. The dense forest growth and very high humidity probably discouraged settlement in this area. Finally, southwest Africa, centering on Namibia, has very low population density. This is the home of the Namib Desert.

## POPULATION DYNAMICS

Africans have large families. Women have five or six children on average. Because their children are their only security in old age, they want large families. Families used to be much larger, particularly in rural farming communities, because children were needed to work on the farms. Also, because the infant mortality—the number of children who die before their first birthday—was high, having many children was necessary. Childlessness was considered a tragedy. Among the Akan of

In the African world, children are a major source of labor. They fetch water, care for younger siblings, work in fields, and help with household chores. One of these children is carrying stones for house construction; the older boy is carrying a table for the local school teacher.

Ghana, a woman who had 10 children would receive a special feast in her honor.

Children are treasured in the African world, and large families are a source of prestige and a sign of God's blessing. As a result, Africa has a very high fertility rate (number of children born to a woman during her lifetime), which has resulted in 46 percent of the population being younger than 15 years of age. In areas of ethnic and political strife, children are seen as a way of securing votes or political power or even as warriors. At home, children work in agricultural fields as herders, care for younger

Alhaji Nassarawa is shown with his three wives in Kano, Nigeria. He has 16 children with his three wives and hopes to have 20. His father had 24 children from his four wives. Polygamy is widely accepted in many parts of Africa, and is the norm in Islam.

siblings, and help with household chores such as fetching water. Many live very hard lives. Only 5 percent of the population is older than 65 years. In the United States, in comparison, children account for only 20 percent of the population younger than 15 years of age and 12 percent of the population is 65 years or older.

Fertility rates tend to be lower in urban areas. Areas with high levels of female literacy also have lower fertility rates. In Kenya, women with secondary or higher education have five children on average compared to seven for those with little or no education.

Family sizes vary quite considerably. Culture, particularly religious belief, is an important factor in family size. In Islam, a man may have up to four wives. Competition among the wives for favor with their husband leads to large families. Thus, Muslims have much larger families than non-Muslims. Let's visit a home in Kano, northern Nigeria.

Alhaji Nassarawa is about 50 years old. A devout Muslim, he has three wives and 16 children. His first wife has eight, the second has five, and the third has three. He hopes to have at least 20 children before he dies. His father had 24 children from his four wives. "My first wife has been very good to me," he explains, "She has given me eight children. My second one has given me only five, but she will give me more. My third wife has been married to me for only five years, but she has given me three children already. I'm a happy man. God has been good to me."

Alhaji Nassarawa's three wives share a common kitchen in the big house where they all live. Their children play and even eat together. Each wife has a separate bedroom that she shares with her children. The wives share household chores and take turns cooking for their husband. All three of them married at age 15. Most women marry young in the Muslim areas of Northern Nigeria. Their husband makes the decision regarding the number of children he wants to have with each of them.

## Life Expectancy and Infant Mortality

Life expectancy in African countries is much lower than in the rest of the world. Because of HIV/AIDS and other diseases, average life expectancy in 2004 was 49 years. In Zimbabwe, Zambia, Malawi, Mozambique, Sierra Leone, and Botswana, life expectancy is less than 40 years. In 2004, the infant mortality rate in the African world was 88, meaning that 88 out of every 1,000 children born were expected to die before their first birthday.

This problem is much worse in countries that are torn by civil war, drought, or other problems. In Sierra Leone, probably the worst place for infants in Africa, 153 out of every 1,000 children born during 2003 were expected to die before their first birthday. In the United States, the number is seven children out of every 1,000 born. For African children, life is very tough. Many children are sent out of the home when they are as young as five years old to earn money to supplement the family income.

Let us stop briefly in Bujumbura, Burundi's national capital, and check in on two friends. Emmanuel Harerimana, age 11, spends his nights in a wrecked car in Bwiza, a slum in the city center. Children of his age on the streets are used as sex partners by the older boys and are sometimes raped. Ndihokubwayo is 13 years old. When his father died, he left his village in Bubanza Province to find a job and a better life in the city. Disappointment swiftly followed: He ended up living on the streets because he could not find work.

Emmanuel and Ndihokubwayo are among thousands of other street children in Burundi's urban centers. Compelled to fend for themselves, they do whatever they can to survive. Some, like Emmanuel, lack proper shelter. The United Nations is working hard to improve life for such children.

## Wabenzi

In direct contrast to the poor street children are the *Wabenzi*. This group has no national boundary. Rather, they are usually found in Africa's urban areas, from Cape Town, South Africa, to Accra, Ghana, from Lagos, Nigeria, to Nairobi, Kenya. *Wabenzi* is a Swahili term that refers to the tribe that drives Mercedes-Benz or BMW vehicles. In some cases, Wabenzi drive their second cars, Pajeros or Range Rovers, which are kept for going on vacation trips or for shopping at the market. They dress in the finest western clothes, with ample jewelry to decorate their hands, wrists, and necks. Their children go to the finest schools locally or in the United States, England, or France. They speak English or French but not their mother tongue. Wabenzi live in huge homes surrounded by electric fences or walls topped by broken glass or spikes to keep burglars out. Some homes are even protected by armed security personnel. As you can see, life in Africa's urban centers is one of major contrasts—extreme wealth and extreme poverty.

## URBANIZATION AND PRIMATE CITIES

Most of sub-Saharan Africa's people live in villages and small towns. Urban dwellers accounted for about 31 percent of the population in 2004, but this number is growing very rapidly. The level of urbanization varies greatly from South Africa, with 53 percent urban, to Ethiopia and Uganda, with 15 percent and 12 percent, respectively. East Africa has lower levels of urbanization (22 percent) than West Africa (36 percent) or Southern Africa (about 50 percent).

When a country's largest city has a population more than double that of the second-largest urban center, it is referred to as a primate city. Most countries in the African world have primate cities. A primate city is not only disproportionately large; it is also the hub of a country's modern development, as well as its social, economic, and often political activity. Examples include Kampala, Uganda's largest city, which is about ten times as large as Jinja, the second-ranked city; Lagos, home to about 60 percent of Nigeria's GNP; and Dar es Salaam, which accounts for more than 50 percent of all manufacturing jobs in Tanzania. Like giants, primate cities gobble up most of the growth and new development in their countries. As a result, they continue to grow bigger and attract more and more people.

## RURAL-TO-URBAN MIGRATION

African cities are growing very rapidly, more rapidly than anywhere else in the world. A primary reason for this rapid urbanization is that rural residents are moving in droves to find jobs, education, health care, and the modern life. These are found only in the modern cities of Africa. Extreme poverty, land shortage, and natural disasters are also factors that "push" people from the countryside. Thus, urban areas are growing more rapidly than industry or employment opportunities. This is called "overurbanization."

Frequently, many of the new urban arrivals lack the education or skills that enable them to get a job in the urban area.

Unemployment is high in rural Africa where most people depend on farming. High population pressure on the land means that increasing numbers of young people have no land for farming and thus, no jobs. At 11:00 in the morning, these young men have no income and nowhere to go. They will ultimately migrate to urban centers in hopes of finding jobs. In the city, they do whatever they can to survive.

Moreover, urban employment is severely limited. Thus, people end up doing whatever they can just to survive. Most people work in the informal sector (such as in petty trade and construction). Still, there are not enough jobs for all these immigrants.

An even more difficult problem is urban housing. There is simply not enough housing for all the people in Africa's cities. The poor build with whatever materials they can find—cardboard, aluminum sheets, wood, and plywood—usually on the outskirts of the city. Such housing is unauthorized. People who live there lack access to simple necessities such as electricity, clean water, and adequate sewage disposal. To see these problems first hand, let us stop in Lagos for a brief visit.

## Lagos, the City of Ordered Chaos

With an estimated metropolitan population of about 14 million in 2004, Lagos is the largest city in the African world and the second largest on the continent (Cairo, Egypt, is the largest). It was Nigeria's capital until 1991, when the capital was moved to Abuja; however Lagos continues to be the commercial and industrial center of Nigeria. By 2020, Lagos's population is expected to reach 24 million people, making it the world's third-largest city.

Oil, natural gas, and coal prop up the economy of Lagos. Between 1965 and 1973, during a boom in world oil prices, the city grew very rapidly. It attracted numerous immigrants from all over West Africa. The 1981 slump in oil prices ended the good times, yet the immigrants continued to arrive daily.

Today, energy and water access, sewage removal, transportation, and housing are severely limited. Although Lagos consumes 45 percent of Nigeria's total energy, "knowing somebody" or paying a bribe is essential for finding basic services such as electricity and water.

Moreover, the electricity supply is not dependable. Power outages that last up to eight hours are common. Nigerians jokingly translate the acronym for the Nigerian Energy and Power Authority (NEPA) as "Never Expect Power Always." Rich people have generators, but crafty people may work together to lay cables and steal electricity from a government building nearby.

Although Lagos is almost surrounded by water, it suffers from an acute and worsening water-supply shortage. The main commercial and administrative center of Lagos is Lagos Island, which is connected to the mainland by three large bridges. On the mainland, unlit highways, mountains of smoldering garbage, and dirt streets weave through numerous slums, where sewers run with raw waste. Much of the city's human waste is dumped into open drains that discharge onto the marshes and lagoons.

Because of Lagos's physical geography and the explosive population growth, transportation within the city is a major headache. It takes an average of two to three hours to travel 5 to 10 miles (8 to 16 kilometers). Three bridges connect about

Traffic jams are a major shopping experience. Before the traffic stops, these children come running from all directions, some as young as 10 or less, carrying all kinds of things for sale—wrist watches, bagged water, hard-boiled eggs, newspapers, insect repellents, and even calculators—tapping on your windows to get your attention. If you show a little interest, they pursue you, darting through chaotic vehicular traffic to clinch the deal. Inhaling fumes from automobile exhausts, and working to avoid being hit by the endless stream of cars, many of these business people make barely $2.00 each day.

2,175 miles (3,500 square kilometers) of lagoon, islands, swamp, and the mainland. As a result, traffic congestion, particularly congested bridges, is a daily problem.

Rush hour in Lagos is an unforgettable experience. About 20 passengers pack into one bus that was built to seat 7. Immediately, the driver grinds into gear and lurches at full throttle to gain a six-inch lead over his competitor. The sideview mirror has to be pulled in for the bus to squeeze through. The action never stops. Blaring horns, screeching brakes, and bellowing smoke everywhere! That is Lagos in motion—a city of miraculous survivors!

In African cities, traffic jams are a key marketplace occurrence. They are almost like shopping malls. When the cars stop, the trading begins. Girls and boys, some barely 10 years old, balance wares on their heads and wade through the traffic to make a sale. Toilet brushes, bread, smoked fish, toothbrushes, insect repellent, clothing, maps, inflatable globes, and even a steering wheel are sold as traffic becomes ever more ensnared. Some services are provided. As the traffic halts, teams of children wash and wipe windshields for a small fee.

Living in the city is difficult, but it comes with some social prestige. Most people feel a desperate need to depend on God for daily survival. Churches are usually filled to capacity, because many people are seeking spiritual solutions to their economic problems. Most Lagos residents want to do more than simply survive; they want capital to start their own business. They do anything just to survive. As they say in Yoruba, "Eko gbole o gbole," meaning "Anything goes in Lagos." Before we leave Lagos, let's take a quick look at some of the things people do. It is almost the same in every African city, and it is called the informal sector.

### The Urban Informal Sector

The urban informal sector is fascinating and universal in the African world. When rain makes a market run with mud, kids wait with buckets of water to wash shoppers' feet for a fee. A man pushes a cart from one home to the next, making $65 per month to haul away garbage. He earns another $55 by salvaging the reusable junk. A tanker pulls up to fill a 100-gallon water tank for $6. The tank owner then sells a bucketful for 9 cents. A teenager in Kampala buys a 100-piece bag of candy for $2 and sells each piece for about 5 cents.

Frequently, the informal sector supplements the formal sector. When the Nigerian government cuts domestic fuel supplies to meet export demands, the informal sector fills the tanks of taxis and buses to keep vehicles moving. Young men rush to fill the tanks of prospective customers with gasoline at three to five times the regular price.

### Transportation in African Cities

Travel in African cities is problematic. Dilapidated minibuses serve the cities and countryside. In Nairobi, Kenya, they are called *matatus*; in Accra, they are called *tro tro*; and in Lagos, they are called *okada*. They are always full but also always seem to have room for more. When someone at the back wants to get off, half the bus must get off first then get back on to continue the journey. The smell of gasoline fumes wafts through the floor. Meanwhile, an irate chicken wrapped in a plastic bag pecks at passengers' feet.

The signs on these minibuses are so fascinating that a whole book could be written about them. Here are a few from Accra, Ghana. Can you understand what they mean?

- God Dey!
- The evil that men do . . .
- Oh God help me!
- Ghana Hard, Still Ghana Hard
- POOR NO FRIEND
- No Where Cool
- LIFE IS WAR
- Heaven gate—No bribe

### Commuting in Cape Town, South Africa

The bus is usually the safest form of transportation in Cape Town. Let us follow Judy as she heads to work today. Because she does not own a car, the 25-year-old schoolteacher relies exclusively on Cape Town's public transportation system to get to work every day. Her home is about 15 miles (25 kilometers) from the high school where she works. Judy has a choice of three modes of transportation to get to work: bus, train, or minibus taxi. She prefers to take the bus, because it is safer than the train and more reliable than the taxi. The journey takes about 45 minutes, and then it is just a short walk to school. There are, however, two small problems. She normally gets soaked when it rains, because there is no bus shelter to cover passengers while they are waiting for the bus. Also, the bus is often full and sometimes she has to stand for most of the journey.

Taking the train is cheaper than the bus, but she has to change at a junction midway through the journey. There is also the problem of robbery. On one occasion when she took the train, all the commuters in her car were robbed of their money by a gang of youths armed with knives. Since then, Judy vowed never to take the train again, but she does sometimes.

The minibus taxi is by far the quickest mode of public transportation available to Judy. She takes it on the rare occasions when she runs late. It takes about 10 minutes less than the bus, although she has to take two taxis to get to school. Taking a taxi costs nearly five times as much as using the bus, and the reckless conduct of the drivers makes the taxi a last resort. Taxis are usually overloaded, with perhaps six people squeezed into seating designed to accommodate four. Sometimes the drivers are drunk or high on drugs. Also, many of the taxis are not roadworthy. Judy has had some bad experiences on the few occasions she took the taxi. Once the passengers got stuck without gasoline and had to wait until the driver found someone passing by to take him to a gas station. On another occasion, she was robbed of all her money by two men who had boarded the taxi as passengers. They demanded people's possessions at gunpoint and left immediately.

With frightening encounters like those experienced by Judy on the taxi and train in mind, which mode of transportation would you choose in South Africa? Be careful, we still have more of the African world to explore.

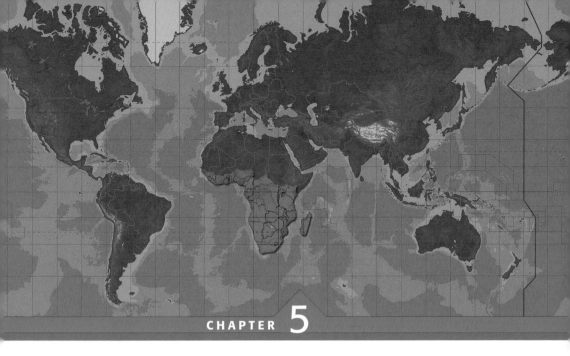

# Culture and Society

The African world is extremely diverse culturally. Africa's population is less than 10 percent of the world's population, but Africans speak about one-third of all the world's languages. Some languages have millions of speakers, and others only a few thousand. Hausa, with more than 50 million speakers, and Yoruba are the two leading languages. Other languages with more than 10 million speakers include Ibo, Swahili, Lingala, and Zulu. About 2,000 distinct languages are spoken in Africa. As a result, language and religion are major sources of conflict in many parts of the region. Because colonialism created multination states and multistate nations, conflict among different language and religious groups is quite common.

## RELIGION

Christianity, Islam, and indigenous (native) religions dominate the African world. The northern parts are mostly Muslim, and southern regions are mostly Christian and animist. The transition zone, across West Africa from Senegal through Nigeria and Sudan all the way to Somalia, is an area of religious conflict.

## Traditional Animism

Before Islam and Christianity arrived, indigenous religions prevailed. There was the almighty god, Onyame among the Akan of Ghana, who created all things. Onyame lives in the sky. He is too holy and powerful for direct human contact. To reach Onyame, humans need intermediaries. This is where the lesser gods come in. Gods and spirits inhabit natural phenomena such as rivers, mountains, rocks, and even some trees. In addition, the dead are alive in the spirit world, waiting to be reborn. Thus, gods and spirits are part of daily life and witness every move and act.

The spirit world is believed to govern human affairs. Spirits can inflict misfortune on the living, especially for misdeeds. For failing to provide a fitting burial, for example, the living may be afflicted with misfortune, sickness, or even death. Failing to take care of the living children of the dead or abusing community property, such as land, can merit similar sanctions. Thus, in the event of misfortune or prolonged sickness, it is critical to consult an *okomfo,* or priest, to inquire about the cause. Offering appropriate sacrifices to the offended spirits usually lifts the curse and ends the suffering.

Annual festivals and celebrations commemorate the living, the dead, and those yet to be born. During public gatherings, libation (drink offering) is poured to invoke the presence of Onyame and ancestral spirits to preside and bless the people. In the event of a national catastrophe, sacrifices are presented to Onyame and the ancestral spirits to appease them and ask for their protection. Periodic sacrifices express thanks to Onyame

The village chief pours libation to invoke the presence and blessing of Onyame and ancestral spirits during a welcome ceremony. Among the Akan of Ghana, hard liquor, schnapps, is preferred for libation. When this is not available, other alcoholic beverages may be substituted such as the Star Beer or Guinness in the foreground.

and the spirits for protection from *Obonsam* (Satan) and *obay-ifo* (witches and wizards). Sacrifices are also appropriate when a person is requesting favor from Onyame or the spirits.

Indigenous African religion was polytheistic (having beliefs in many gods) and included a belief in reincarnation. Prosperity in this life was a sign of favor from the spirits. The elaborate systems of spiritual sanctions (curses or blessings) helped maintain social order. The system, however, clashed fundamentally with Islam and Christianity when those faiths arrived.

## Islam

Islam arrived in Africa during the seventh century. Followers of Islam, called Muslims, believe that Muhammad, the founder, was the last in a long line of prophets that include Abraham, Moses, and Jesus Christ. The Islamic holy book, the Koran, is the word of Allah (God) revealed to Muhammad. It contains instructions for daily living.

Muslims are required to pray five times daily facing Mecca (in Saudi Arabia) and to give alms. In addition, if at all possible, they must go on a pilgrimage (*hajj*) to Mecca at least once in their lifetime. Those who have undertaken this pilgrimage take the title *Alhaji*. (Do you remember our friend Alhaji Nassarawa in Kano from Chapter 4?) Finally, in addition to repetition of the basic creed, Muslims fast during daytime hours for a period of 30 days each year (*Ramadan*). Doing these things faithfully may not guarantee heaven at death. For a Muslim who dies in a *jihad* (holy war), especially while spreading Islam, heaven is guaranteed.

## Christianity

Christianity emphasizes belief in one God and salvation through God's son, Jesus Christ. Salvation is not based on what a person does but on faith in Christ. A person dies once, unlike in indigenous African religion, and then faces eternal hell or heaven. Those who believe in Jesus Christ are guaranteed to go to heaven, but those who do not supposedly go to hell. Good deeds, although encouraged, are not required (as in Islam) to reach heaven. To receive forgiveness, a person has to confess his or her sins to God and ask for forgiveness.

Christianity came to northeastern Africa, modern Sudan, and Ethiopia first. The Ethiopian Orthodox Church, the state church of the ancient Ethiopian kingdom, continues today. Christianity spread through the continent in the nineteenth century, when European and American missionaries became established in West Africa. From there, it spread through Central and Southern Africa. Christian missionaries provided health care and education as inducements to conversion.

Today, Christianity is growing rapidly in the African world, and Christians are either the majority or a substantial minority in each country. The Anglican Church has been growing so rapidly in Kenya, Uganda, and Nigeria that, by 2000, there were more Anglicans in these countries combined than in the United Kingdom, where the Anglican Church started. The African Anglican church maintains the conservative church doctrine, opposing the ordination of homosexuals and women as priests, for example.

Independent African churches that combine elements of Christianity and traditional African religion have also emerged. Examples include the Zionists in South Africa and Cherubim and Seraphim in West Africa.

### The Prosperity Gospel

In the large urban centers of the African world, a new gospel has emerged: the prosperity gospel. This is an adaptation of Evangelical Christian doctrine mixed with elements of traditional African religion. It has a simple message: Jesus Christ died to set all people free from poverty and disease. Lasting freedom from poverty and disease can only be found in Jesus Christ. Let's stop briefly at the Miracle Center in Kinshasa, Democratic Republic of the Congo.

The huge church building is bursting at the seams with perhaps 2,000 people. They are singing, dancing, and praying—everybody at once—at the top of their voices. Some are crying, jumping, waving their hands, kneeling, or lying prostrate on the floor. After about 10 minutes, the pastor steps to the microphone and everybody is quiet. "Jesus died, that you might live,"

Dancing pervades African culture and may be observed everywhere—at church services, festivals, weddings, or even funerals such as this one in Kumasi, Ghana. The clothing is also symbolic—dark colors such as black, red, and brown are for mourning and sorrow. For Christian funerals, however, white is preferred. White symbolizes joy, an end to suffering and entry into God's rest for the departed, and thus rejoicing for those left behind.

he says. "He suffered that you may enjoy abundant life. Jesus died for you. Somebody say Amen! You don't have to be sick. You don't have to be poor. The Bible says that God will bless those who give to Him. What do you need? A job? A husband? A baby? Healing? Jesus is here! Give generously, and expect your miracle."

The crowd is electrified. They charge forward with dancing to bring their gifts. They give almost everything, cell phones, clothing, wristwatches, and especially money. One woman gave her whole monthly salary in hope that she will have a child. Why have such churches emerged? In traditional African religion, sacrificial gifts to ancestors and spirits were required to secure protection and blessing. Trapped in poverty, many people flock to the hope that such churches provide. For those who are new to the city, the church family and its activities fill the void of loneliness and isolation.

## Religion and Conflict

Religious conflict is a major problem in the African countries that have large religious minorities. In Sudan, the northern part of the country is Muslim and the southern part is Christian and animist. The pro-Muslim government based in the north imposed *sharia* (Islamic law), as the law of the land. Under sharia, a person who steals may have one hand cut off. Adultery is punished with death by stoning. Public punishment by caning for misdemeanors is common. Christians also are required to live under this law.

No country is more torn by religious conflict than Nigeria. In the northern part, where Islam dominates, some states have adopted sharia in defiance of the Nigerian federal government. In 2004 in Kaduna, a young woman was sentenced to death by stoning for engaging in sexual relations outside marriage. Not all residents of Kaduna are Muslim, and the religious minorities' opposition to the sharia law has led to religious riots. Many people have died as result of these conflicts.

## ADORNMENT AND SYMBOLISM

Modes of dressing vary throughout the African world. A person's status, age, and mood can be gauged quite accurately from clothing. Among the Akan of Ghana, red, black, and dark brown are mourning colors and are worn during times of grief. White symbolizes joy, success, or victory. During formal occasions, Africans like to dress up. An Akan chief portrays his authority by his clothing, gold ornaments, and symbols of office.

The Tuareg, a people who live in northern parts of West Africa from Senegal, Mali, Burkina Faso, Niger, and Nigeria, call themselves *Kel tagelmust*, meaning "the people of the veil." The men wear veils instead of the women. A 10- to 20-foot (3- to 6-meter) veil preserves a man's dignity by hiding his emotions. The Tuareg consider it shameful if strangers or those of higher status see a man's mouth. Most shameful is if his mother-in-law sees his mouth. The veil also keeps sand out of a man's nose and mouth. His breath is trapped in the veil, protecting his lungs from the dry Saharan air with moisture. Because it is wound thickly around his head, the veil keeps away flies and even acts as a sunshade.

In African textiles, symbols and fabrics also make a clear statement. Each motif has a name derived from proverbs or historical events. Among the Asante, a ceremonial cloth called *kente,* which is handwoven on a treadle loom, is full of symbolism. Four-inch-wide strips of dazzling, multicolored, bold patterns and geometric shapes are sewn together into larger, colorful pieces. Each pattern has its own meaning. Here are two examples.

*Wofro dua pa a na ye pia wo* literally means "a person who climbs a worthy tree deserves help." This expresses the Akan social value that a person who undertakes a worthy task deserves support from the community. The rest of the society expects to benefit from this worthy cause and so should help. This cloth symbolizes aspiration, mutual benefit, and sharing.

*Obaakofo mmu oman* means "one person does not rule a nation." It expresses the Akan political system, which is based on a council of elders and participatory democracy. The Akan political system frowns on dictatorship. The cloth symbolizes participatory democracy and warns against autocratic rule or dictatorship.

## FAMILY

In traditional African society, marriage is a union of two families not just of two individuals. Thus, your brother or sister may not marry your wife's brother or sister. That is considered

Children are treasured in African society and are a sign of God's favor. Childless adults are despised. In many African countries children younger than 15 comprise at least 40 percent of the population. These children are fascinated with a video replay of their play captured on tape. Secure and safe, children usually play outdoors unaccompanied by adults.

incest, just as marrying your own sister or brother would be. Also, in parts of Africa, polygamy is permitted—a man may have more than one wife. In the event of conflict between husband and wife, family members, especially the parents of the couple, are expected to mediate. Frequently, such intervention is enough to stop a divorce.

Children are treasured in African society. Marrying and having children is a sign of social respectability and God's favor. Unmarried and childless adults are despised. Also, children belong to the extended family not just to the couple. In patrilineal societies, the children belong to the father's family and inherit from him, and in matrilineal societies they belong to the mother's and inherit from her. Dual inheritance, inheriting from both mother and father, is rare in African society.

Sharing with relatives, particularly siblings, is required in African society. The way to display wealth is to provide generously for poorer family members. Poverty is a sign of misfortune or bad luck, and the rich are expected to help. A person is not supposed to put a monetary value on such assistance because this same assistance would be provided to him or her if it was needed. If a man's brother dies, it is customary for that man to take care of his brother's wife and children. In some areas, this translates into marrying the wife of the deceased.

Aging is a sign of maturity, experience, and wisdom. Younger members of the family are expected to provide for the aged. Those who do not are looked down on and become social outcasts. A proverb from the Akan people of Ghana says, "Because your parents took care of you while you were cutting your teeth, you must take care of them while their teeth fall out." It is normal for parents to live with their grown children and grandchildren. Family support is the only form of "social security."

Political allegiance is first to the immediate extended family, then to the community, and then to the tribe or ethnic group. Allegiance to the country has low priority. This partially explains why African leaders surround themselves with family members or people from their ethnic or tribal group. Society expects a person to use his position to improve the livelihoods of relatives. In American society, this is seen as nepotism.

Traditional cultural values are changing rapidly. Increased migration from rural to urban areas means that aged parents now often live alone in rural poverty. Nursing homes are not yet widely accepted but probably will be in the future. Also, HIV/AIDS has exhausted the traditional safety net of family support. Increasingly, young AIDS orphans live alone in their parents' home with little adult support or supervision.

## Cost of Funerals

Funerals are profoundly important and occasions for celebration in many African cultures. They are creative and colorful and can be very expensive. Let us visit a funeral in Accra, Ghana. It is a Saturday afternoon. About 400 people, coworkers, neighbors, relatives, and even strangers have gathered together for Holala Nortey's funeral. The 63-year-old man was a taxi driver at a hotel in Accra for 30 years before he died of a stroke. He left behind four children and ten grandchildren. He had used an old Mercedes-Benz sedan most of his career, and when he died, his relatives decided to honor him by burying him in a replica of one. A Mercedes-Benz coffin would symbolize his love for his work.

The coffin itself is immaculate in its detail. The four-door wooden Mercedes includes windshield wipers, rearview and sideview mirrors (with real glass), an antenna, a Mercedes-Benz hood emblem, an exhaust pipe, and tags (GG7155). The coffin alone cost $450, and family members estimate that the funeral ultimately will cost about $1,400. This is a huge expenditure in a country where most people earn less than one dollar per day.

Family elders placed Holala's body in the Mercedes-Benz coffin, along with jewelry and other items that were supposed to go with him to the grave. The pallbearers carried the coffin down the rugged road leading to the public cemetery, sunlight glinting off of the Mercedes-Benz's white paint. The family hopes that, satisfied with this funeral, Holala will send blessings, not curses, from the spirit world.

## NAMES

Before you leave this discussion of African culture, you must have an African name. Children are given names in very elaborate ceremonies. Because a person's name is believed to influence his or her character, great care and thought go into name selection. Naming ceremonies and preferred names vary across the continent.

In Kenya, a child's name depends on the circumstances of birth. Among the Luo, a child born in the afternoon is called *Ochieng.* The female alternative is *Achieng.* The child has another name from the father. At baptism, a Christian name may also be assigned.

In the Democratic Republic of the Congo, the maternal uncle chooses the name of a boy, and the mother or aunts name a girl. In that culture, newborn babies are not considered to be truly persons until they are named.

Among the Asante of Ghana, the day of birth gives a child one name. A female baby born on Sunday is called *Esi,* and a male is called *Kwesi.* Thus, Kofi Annan, United Nations Secretary-General, is a male child born on Friday. A female child born on Friday is called *Afua.*

## MARRIAGE

Next to funerals, marriage is the most celebrated social event. In the past, families arranged most marriages. This practice is less common today. When a couple marries, the man usually pays a "bride price" to the bride's parents. He can demand his money back if the marriage ends in divorce. Couples may have more than one marriage ceremony. In addition to the traditional exchange of gifts between families, there may be a civil ceremony in which vows are exchanged. Finally, the couple may have a Christian church ceremony. Wedding celebrations involve singing, dancing, and feasting and may last for many days. The living, the dead, and those yet to be born all participate.

## CULTURE AND CONFLICT

Cultural conflicts are widespread throughout the African world. Frequently, beyond the most visible issues of religious or language differences lie long-standing conflicts over resources such as land. In the Darfur region of Sudan, competition over land and water underlies long-standing tensions between Arab camel herders and African subsistence farmers.

Those tensions have led to a terrifying civil war. Arab militias backed by the Sudanese government have chased Africans off of their land in what United Nations officials have called a campaign of "ethnic cleansing."

Nigeria has an extremely volatile history of ethnic conflict. In Jos, 1,000 people were killed during religious riots in 2001. In northern Nigeria, in the politically volatile town of Kano, about 20,000 Christians fled their homes during recent riots. In May 2004, a conflict resulted in a death toll ranging from an official figure of 67 to residents' estimates of up to 10 times that number. Whatever the number, the consequences are widespread. Thousands of Muslims and Christians fled in opposite directions. Towns and villages in Plateau State have become Christian-only or Muslim-only enclaves.

The attacks are fueled less by religious passions than by deep-seated rivalries over land and power. Competition for political power has hardened ethnic and religious divides. As land has become scarcer, feuds between farmers and cattle herders have turned deadly. The people who call themselves indigenous to this region are mostly Christians and farmers, and those they classify as settlers are mostly Muslim cattle herders and traders from the Hausa and Fulani tribes.

## Côte d'Ivoire: Ethnic Conflict or Fighting for Land

In the world's largest cocoa-producing country, several years of civil war have produced an ugly ethnic feud over cocoa land. The war, which broke out in September 2002, is officially over, but peace remains elusive. The largely northern and immigrant workers who cultivate cocoa in Côte d'Ivoire have been expelled from their plantations. Deadly reprisal attacks have followed. In the countryside, particularly across the cocoa belt, massacres and expulsions continue. At the heart of the war is the contest over cocoa land. Tensions have brewed for years as cultivatable land dwindled, the population swelled, and immigrants from Burkina Faso and Mali poured in. Some newcomers worked as sharecroppers and hired hands and eventually bought large plantations.

Today, roughly a quarter of Côte d'Ivoire's 16 million people, including those born there to immigrant parents, are considered foreigners. For years, those who considered themselves natives resented the prospering immigrants. Once war broke out, clashes between natives and foreigners intensified. Under current law, only Ivorians can own land, so immigrant landowners hide to avoid being killed. They have become beggars. Among them is Yaya Koné, the son of migrants from Burkina Faso. Koné, now 55, was born in Côte d'Ivoire. He worked on other people's land for many years and saved enough to buy his own 10-acre plantation.

One day, two young villagers knocked on his door and said, "We don't need you any more. Your people brought war to this country. Go home." He had neither the time nor the nerve to argue. Within minutes, a village mob arrived. His longtime neighbors emptied and then burned his house. Koné and dozens of fellow immigrants fled. He suspects that his neighbors have cleaned out his cocoa harvest, and he is too frightened to return. He remains in hiding, living hand to mouth, in this bustling cocoa trading town, hoping that one day he will return to his cocoa plantation. Going to Burkina Faso is not an option. "I'm too old," Koné said. "My plantation is here."

We now leave Africa's rich and turbulent culture to explore the region's political history. Before we move on to the next chapter, however, have you chosen an African name?

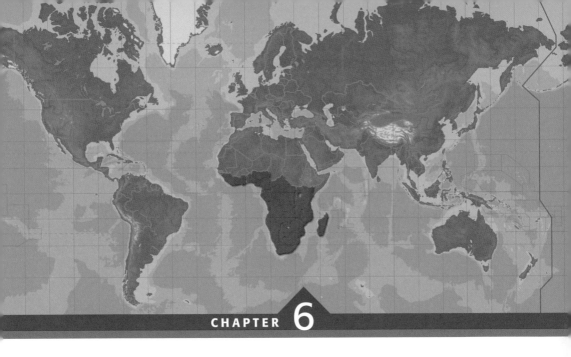

# CHAPTER 6

# Political History

More than four decades after winning independence, many countries in the African world are worse off than they were at independence. This chapter attempts to explain what happened by tracing the path taken by African world countries from their independence from colonial powers to dependence on the World Bank and International Monetary Fund (IMF).

Most African countries attained independence in 1960. Initially, joy and optimism were very high. At long last, Africans were going to govern Africans. They were going to be masters of their own destiny, and they were going to develop quickly and catch up with the rest of the world. A decade later, much of the optimism had faded. In the 1980s, decline set in. Famine, war, poverty, and debt became the headlines. In the 1990s, "crisis" became the region's buzzword—HIV/AIDS crisis, food crisis, debt crisis. In the decade beginning in 2000, the African world is at the crossroads; conditions can improve or they may get much worse. What went wrong? Let us begin with the Organization of African Unity (OAU).

## FROM ORGANIZATION OF AFRICAN UNITY TO AFRICAN UNION

Ghana's first president, Kwame Nkrumah, dreamed of a United States of Africa. Once Ghana attained independence, Nkrumah set out to build a country that was free from poverty, ignorance, and disease. This was a first step toward liberating the rest of Africa from the shackles of colonialism. Africa must unite because a united Africa was the only hope for survival. In 1958, the first conference of independent African states was held in Accra, Ghana. In 1959, Ghana, Guinea, and Mali agreed to unite. This plan was never implemented.

After many states achieved independence in 1960, they began to disagree. Some countries were concerned with protecting their newly won sovereignty. They argued for mutual recognition of equality and sovereignty, noninterference, and economic, cultural, and scientific cooperation. Others, led by Nkrumah, still wanted a United States of Africa patterned after the United States of America. In 1963, the Organization of African Unity (OAU) was formed. An initial goal was to unite Africa and especially to support African countries that were still struggling for independence.

In its 40-year existence, the OAU actively supported Mozambique and Angola as they fought for independence from Portuguese rule. It mediated disputes between neighboring states and supported South African blacks as they fought against apartheid. Because of the noninterference agreement, however, the OAU was unable to stop or resolve destructive civil wars and conflicts such as Somalia, Rwanda, Liberia, and Sierra Leone.

In 2002, the OAU was reborn as the African Union (AU). A major goal of the AU is to promote economic development and ensure effective government. African leaders promise to deliver good governance, peace, and security in exchange for increased foreign investment. Unfortunately, the AU lacks the power to intervene in sovereign African nations or remove repressive leaders.

## FROM POLITICAL PROMISE TO POLITICAL CHAOS

After the short period of euphoria after independence came the long struggle for economic independence and sovereignty. Many governments faced a rising tide of expectations with little or no resources to meet them and very little time to respond. Impatience soon began to set in. Many Africans felt that the political leadership had changed but that their physical and practical circumstances had not. They began to accuse the African leaders of inefficiency, corruption, and incompetence.

Faced with increasing criticism in difficult circumstances, many regimes opted for single-party states to prevent dissent. Political dissent was frequently crushed. The idea was "to work together in unity to build our nation, not against each other to tear it apart." After this, institutions such as the civil service, trade unions, and the military were typically brought under close control and decision making tended to be centralized with fewer people.

In some countries, the democratically elected government manipulated the political apparatus to stifle political dissent and ban opposition parties. This happened in Côte d'Ivoire, where Félix Houphouët-Boigny became president for life. He single-handedly decided and moved the national capital from Abidjan to his hometown, Yamoussoukro, in the interior of the country.

In some countries, a leader's charisma prevented any viable opposition from emerging. Kwame Nkrumah in Ghana and Jomo Kenyatta in Kenya were identified with independence so much that they were seen as "Father of the Nation."

Moreover, African leaders usually tried to keep themselves in power and to rule for life. They used all kinds of practices, including bribery and intimidation, to sustain their rule indefinitely. In Zambia, Kenneth Kaunda ruled as president from 1964 to 1991. Similarly, Julius Nyerere ruled Tanzania from 1961 to 1984 and Hastings Kamuzu Banda ruled Malawi from 1964 until 1994, when he was voted out of power. In the Democratic Republic of the Congo, Mobutu Sese Seko ruled as president from 1965 until Laurent Kabila overthrew him in another coup in 1995.

Frustrated with their circumstances and with no end in sight, the people instigated a time of forced political change. Military coups became commonplace. In some countries, the one-party state began as a military regime, which perpetuated itself in power. No country illustrates these developments better than Ghana under Kwame Nkrumah.

### Kwame Nkrumah and Ghana: From Grace to Grass

Immediately after Ghana won independence, Nkrumah began several major development projects designed to make Ghana the star of Africa. A national airline, Ghana Airways, and a national shipping company, Black Star Line, were established. The Akosombo Dam was built to provide hydroelectric power. An aluminum-smelting project, Volta Aluminum Company, was begun, although the terms were not favorable for Ghana. The Kwame Nkrumah University of Science and Technology was established to provide training in science, engineering, pharmacy, agriculture, and architecture, among other things. Education at all levels was expanded, and primary education became compulsory and free. Health services were expanded, with many new hospitals and clinics and two teaching hospitals.

To develop Ghana fully and immediately, Nkrumah opted for state socialism. Socialist experts, state farms, and state-owned industries were the standard. Nkrumah maintained that

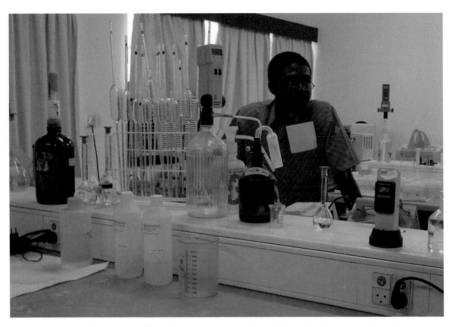

Science and technology education continue to be a key, but frequently under-funded, need in many African countries. Frequently, equipment and supplies are received as donations from more economically developed countries. This photo shows the environmental research laboratory at the University of Ghana in the Department of Geography and Resources.

state ownership of production was the main strategy for Ghana's industrialization. He crushed opposition severely, and opposition leaders who were not jailed fled into exile. By 1964, Ghana had "chosen" to become a one-party state. Corruption, nepotism, and discrimination were rampant. Then the world price of cocoa, Ghana's main export, fell drastically. Unable to pay its debts and faced with shortage of consumer items such as sugar, flour, soap, milk, drugs, and spare automobile parts, the country faced economic disaster. Conditions were ripe for a change of government, and this happened on February 24, 1966. For the next quarter-century, Ghana had almost a revolving-door military rule that periodically was interspersed with brief civilian regimes. Instead of economic growth and prosperity, Ghanaians experienced massive poverty and huge declines in almost every aspect of life.

Unfortunately, Ghana's story is not unique. Between 1960 and 2002, the African world had 85 successful military coups in 35 countries and numerous unsuccessful ones. By 1995, Ghana had experienced five military coups and 25 of its 38 years of independence had been under military rule. Nigeria had spent 25 of its 35 years under five different military regimes. Uganda, Benin, Burkina Faso, and Sudan had each experienced five military coups. Sierra Leone and Lesotho had each experienced three coups. Even Madagascar experienced a military coup in 1972.

Most countries that had not experienced military coups by 1990 were governed by one-party governments, dictatorships, or perpetual leaders ("leaders for life," as they were called). Most leaders viciously crushed any opposition. Often, the one-party state functioned like a police state with socialist rhetoric. In Zimbabwe, Robert Mugabe continues this tradition. He has kept himself in power through intimidation and widespread human rights abuses and by mercilessly crushing the opposition.

Not all African countries have experienced the history of military coups. Senegal and Tanzania have had smooth transitions of power without military coups.

## THINGS FALL APART

Some countries began to unravel and fall apart immediately after winning independence. As noted before, artificial political boundaries were imposed under colonialism. Thus, after independence, secessionist (breakaway) movements emerged in many countries and in some cases continue today. The Democratic Republic of the Congo (DRC) provides an excellent illustration.

In the DRC, chaos ensued almost immediately after independence was achieved in 1960. After exploiting the country for years, the Belgians, suddenly declared the DRC independent without making any transition arrangements. Immediately, there was a power struggle to fill the vacuum. Katanga, a mineral-rich province, attempted to secede right away. A year later, the prime minister, Patrice Lumumba, was seized and killed by troops loyal to army Chief Joseph Mobutu. In 1965, Mobutu seized power and renamed the country Zaire and himself Mobutu Sese Seko. Under his rule, "Zaire" became synonymous with "corruption." The fighting continues today. The country's vast mineral wealth is a major reason for the fighting. All the factions are taking advantage of the anarchy to plunder the abundant natural resources including diamonds, cobalt, and crude oil.

In Nigeria, the Ibos attempted to secede and establish the Republic of Biafra. This led to the Biafran War (1967–1970), in which more than one million people were killed. The war caused major disruption and displacement for many people.

Eritrea, formerly a colony of Italy, became part of Ethiopia in 1952. In 1961, Eritrea began to fight for independence. Despite Soviet assistance, Ethiopia could not crush the Eritrean resistance, and the Ethiopian government collapsed in 1991. The new government organized a referendum on the independence of Eritrea in 1993, which resulted in a 99 percent vote for independence. A month later, Eritrea was free.

After five years of peaceful coexistence, Eritrea and Ethiopia went to war over disputed land. Ethiopia needed an outlet to the sea, and Eritrea was not willing to give that. The two-year war cost more than 100,000 lives, displaced thousands from their homes, and diverted much-needed resources from development. In the end, Eritrea had its way, and Ethiopia is now a landlocked territory. This is one more example of the fracturing of the continent.

## ECONOMIC DEVELOPMENT POLICIES

Although all African countries hoped to achieve economic development at the time of independence, they took considerably different courses to attain that goal. Some countries, including Kenya and Côte d'Ivoire, pursued a capitalist strategy. They emphasized economic growth rather than equity in their development strategy. Both domestic and foreign private investments were encouraged and welcomed.

In other countries, capitalism was rejected as being exploitative, inhumane, and contrary to the traditional African values of cooperation and sharing. In these countries, African socialism was the preferred alternative. The goal was to ensure equitable distribution of the results of development. Ghana and Tanzania are the best examples of this approach. In such countries, the state initiated and undertook expensive projects, usually with foreign loans. State farms that employ thousands of people were established to increase agricultural production. In Ghana under Nkrumah, foreigners were invited to invest in industry and commercial enterprise. In order to ensure socialism and prevent the emergence of a local capitalist class, however, Ghanaians were restricted to only petty trading and retailing. They could buy in bulk and resell products, such as cigarettes or sugar, in small packages, usually without permanent shops.

In Mozambique, Angola, and Ethiopia, Afro-Marxism was the development ideology. State farms and factories were established with Soviet and Cuban assistance. The fall of the Soviet Union as a superpower meant the fall of these economies as well. Their dependence on the Soviet Union was no longer sustainable.

## REASONS FOR POLITICAL INSTABILITY

Europeans often handpicked new African leaders who would not challenge colonial interests. Independence also started with European-inspired constitutions that were not based on African realities and experience.

In traditional African society, government was usually by consensus based on unanimity. The council of elders would discuss conflicting viewpoints until they unanimously agreed on one idea. The idea of an opposition is foreign and cannot be translated into many African languages. Thus, "opposition" usually translates into "enemy." It is often difficult to negotiate with one's enemy; rather, one tries to eliminate the opposition.

In many countries, foreign powers supported African despots and kept them in power. The United States and France, for example, sent armies to quell rebellion against Mobutu's dictatorship in the DRC.

The 1990s brought significant change to Africa's political landscape. Responding to the winds of political change, particularly the fall of Communism, many Africans began to agitate for more responsible government and elimination of human rights abuses. The International Monetary Fund (IMF) and World Bank began to make effective governance a condition for continued financial assistance. Repressive governments were increasingly denied aid. In this climate, political leaders were successfully voted out of office in Zambia, Benin, and Madagascar.

In some countries, however, the drive to democratic rule has not been successful. In the DRC, for example, after removing Mobutu from power, Kabila's government could not effectively control the country. Rebel forces sponsored by Rwanda and Uganda occupied large areas of eastern and northern Congo. These two countries had interest in the DRC because of ethnic ties. To guarantee his hold on power, Kabila asked for and obtained military assistance from Angola, Namibia, and Zimbabwe. Kabila was assassinated in 2001, and his son, Joseph Kabila, was sworn in as the next ruler. The conflict in the DRC is far from over, however, because the government has no control over large regions of the country.

## IMF/WORLD BANK VERSUS THE OAU

In 1980, African leaders came together under the OAU to find solutions to Africa's many problems. After lengthy discussions, they agreed to place the blame on foreign nations. Africa was poor, they decided, because of all the bad things that foreigners, especially developed nations, had done, including slavery and colonialism. Also, the developed nations did not treat African nations fairly in trade. As a result, the only solution was for African countries to cooperate with each other, through trade, for example. The final document, called the Lagos Plan of Action (LPA), called for the establishment of an African Economic Community by 2000.

A year later, the World Bank released a report about the true causes of Africa's problems. It placed much blame on African leaders, many of whom were corrupt and mismanaged their countries' economies. For example, state-owned industries were losing money instead of making a profit because of poor management and corruption. They had too many workers who did little, if any, work but were paid monthly. The only solution was to stop the mismanagement and corruption.

Thus, the World Bank set some requirements. Excess workers must be laid off. Government-owned industries must be sold. African countries should produce more, export more, and devalue their currency. Finally, they should pass laws to remove trade barriers and attempt to attract foreign investment in their economies. These were some of the conditions of the Structural Adjustment Program (SAP). Countries that agreed to these conditions received specially negotiated loans and grants from the World Bank and the IMF. Performance was reviewed periodically to evaluate progress on the required economic reforms and the economy.

The SAP requirements were very harsh. Devaluation meant reducing the value of the currency. Exports became cheaper, but imported goods were more expensive. Thus, African countries paid more for imports such as gasoline, food, and medicine but were paid less for their produce such as cocoa and coffee. Also, many people employed by the government were laid off. Government subsidies on health care and education were removed, which increased the cost of education and health care drastically.

Because conditions were deteriorating rapidly—disasters, poverty, and famine all were increasing—many African leaders adopted the SAP instead of LPA. In 1983, Ghana became one of the first countries to adopt the SAP. Still, the problems did not go away; rather, they got worse. In 1981, shortly before the adoption of SAP, 43 percent of Ghana's population was poor. By 1986, it had increased to 54 percent and in 1997, 55 percent of Ghana's population was poor. What should African nations do?

In 1985, the OAU admitted that internal factors such as corruption were partly responsible for Africa's development crisis. External factors, including unfair trade and high interest rates, were also important contributing factors. The OAU emphasized "shared responsibilities." Nevertheless, the World Bank and IMF continued to insist on SAP.

In 1989, the OAU produced another document. This time, it insisted that previous domestic failures were a factor but that SAP was bad for African countries. It increased poverty and income inequality between genders and among ethnic groups. If something was not done quickly, they warned, total economic breakdown would occur. African leaders must ensure good governance and reduce corruption if development is to occur.

In 2000, the World Bank admitted that SAP had problems. Thus, long-term solutions based on partnership between donors and African governments, rather than on force, were necessary. Also, effective government without corruption is required.

Finally, that same year, the OAU came out with a new proposal: New Economic Partnership for Africa's Development (NEPAD). African leaders promised to deliver good governance, peace, and security in exchange for increased foreign investment. Under NEPAD, African leaders accepted blame for nearly all of the problems and nearly all the responsibility for sorting them out.

The World Bank and IMF will reward "good" African governments with grants, loans, and other developmental assistance. It looks as if the World Bank /IMF and African countries finally agree. The new goal is to work together toward achieving the goal of a more economically stable African world.

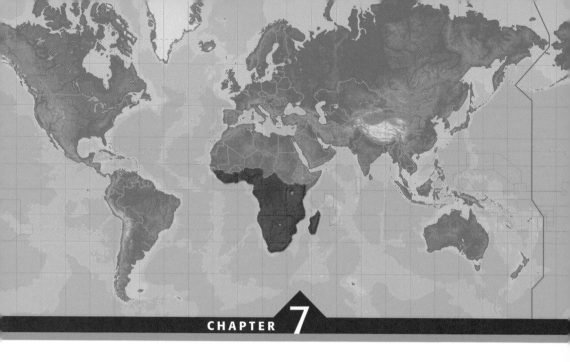

# CHAPTER 7

# Making a Living

Many African people are poorer today than they were in the 1960s. Instead of finding the rapid economic development they anticipated at independence, many people are desperately seeking relief from the grinding poverty and wars that affect their lives. Drought conditions have produced widespread food shortages, forcing many areas to depend on outside food aid. Wood, the main source of fuel for most people, is scarce. Most countries are deeply in debt. Why has this happened? Is it because of lack of natural resources? Is it because of economic mismanagement, as the IMF and World Bank assert? Or is it because of natural circumstances such as drought? This chapter discusses the African world's economic realities, problems, and prospects.

## NATURAL RESOURCES, DEVELOPMENT, AND POVERTY

Natural resources such as gold, diamonds, and oil are important assets for economic development. Countries that lack oil must import it, but those that have this vital resource can sell it and make a profit. Fortunately, many African countries are blessed with huge stores of precious natural resources, including diamonds, oil, gold, and other precious minerals. Few of the resource-rich countries are prospering, however. Sadly, for millions of people in Sierra Leone, Angola, and the Democratic Republic of the Congo, natural resources have produced war, rape, amputations, chaos, and poverty. Before going further, let's look at the natural resource endowment of the African world.

Despite an abundance of natural resources, most African world people live in poverty. According to the World Bank's World Development Report, only six countries in the region had a per capita income of more than $1,000 during 2002. These were Botswana with $3,300, South Africa with $3,020, Gabon with $3,180, Namibia with $2,050, and Cape Verde and Swaziland with $1,330 and $1,290, respectively. In most countries, the annual income per person was less than $500. Most people in the African world live on less than one dollar per day. In fact, for Sierra Leone, a country plagued by conflict, the GNP per capita in 2002 was a mere $130. African countries may be rich in natural resources, but most are controlled by American and European companies that profit from these resources.

### Rich in Oil, yet Very Poor

According to experts, Africa is the world's fastest-growing oil exploration and production zone. The IMF estimates that the region currently earns nearly 30 billion dollars per year from oil exports. Yet, in African countries that sell millions of barrels of oil every year, most people remain mired in poverty. More important, competition over the "black gold" is a source of conflict. Oil brings corruption and war, and, frequently, the revenues are abused and wasted.

Life for the urban poor is difficult. Most people live on $1.00 a day in poor housing. Notice the open drainage and potholes filled with water, an ideal habitat for mosquitoes and other disease-causing organisms. Poor access to clean water and poor sanitation practices combine to make infant mortality high in such areas.

Apart from Gabon, none of the major oil-producing countries in the region has a strong economy. Despite having huge oil revenues, Nigeria and Angola remain poor because of corruption and internal conflict. In fact, gasoline shortages are commonplace in Nigeria, even though the country is the world's seventh-leading producer of oil! The Niger Delta region, the hub of Nigerian oil production, is always an area of political strife and uncertainty. For these Africans countries, oil may be more a curse than a blessing. Could this also be true for diamonds?

## Mineral Wealth

The African world is blessed with abundant natural resources, including coal in Nigeria and Southern Africa and oil and gas in Western Africa (particularly Nigeria) and also Gabon and Angola. Iron and manganese are found in Western and Southern

Africa, and most of the world's known deposits of chromium are found in Zimbabwe and South Africa. Zambia's copper belt and the southern Democratic Republic of the Congo (DRC) boast huge reserves of copper. Ghana and other West African countries have gargantuan amounts of bauxite, the ore from which aluminum is made. Gold abounds in several countries, including Ghana, Zimbabwe, and South Africa. In fact, South Africa has about half of the world's total gold reserves. Botswana is the world's leading producer of gem diamonds. Other important diamond producers include the DRC, Sierra Leone, Namibia, and South Africa.

### Diamonds and Conflict

The curse of resources seems to be even truer for diamonds than for oil. Almost all diamond-producing countries have experienced political instability and war. Fighting is usually over control of the diamond mines, and diamonds fund the wars. This is true in the DRC, Sierra Leone, and Angola.

Although very rich in natural resources, especially diamonds, the DRC is among the world's poorest countries. Mobutu Sese Seko, a ruthless and corrupt dictator, ruled Congo from 1965 until 1997. During his time in office, Seko amassed a fortune of 8 billion dollars in personal wealth. Now, years later, armies from seven different countries plunder and fight—not for the good of the Congolese but as part of a latter-day scramble for Africa and its resource wealth. They fight for the DRC's rich stores of diamonds, gold, and other minerals. By 2004, more than 4 million people had died from massacres, famine, and disease. Although recent treaties have calmed the fighting, the environment is tense and very fragile.

Sierra Leone is another diamond-rich, yet economically poor country that has been ravaged by civil war. Led by Foday Sankoh, the rebel Revolutionary United Front (RUF) fought Sierra Leone government troops from 1991 to 2002. To fund the war, RUF gained control of most of Sierra Leone's diamond-mining areas. They conducted a vicious campaign that spared no one. Men, women, and even babies had legs and hands chopped off. Thousands of women and young girls were abducted, beaten, raped, and used as sex slaves. By 1994, half of Sierra Leone's 4.5 million people had been displaced from their homes and more than 50,000 people had been killed.

In Angola, a civil war funded with diamonds has left more than one million people dead and about 3.5 million people (one-third of the country's population) displaced. Nearly half the country is covered with an estimated 15 million land mines, resulting in the world's highest amputee rate. More than 70,000 people have lost at least one limb. Despite fertile soils and good rains, devastation from famine is widespread. Yet the diamond trade goes on.

Armed conflicts have devastated vast areas rich in resources. During the chaos of war, normal economic activities are disrupted or halted completely. It doesn't have to be that way. Diamonds do not have to produce turmoil and poverty. Botswana's experience tells a different story of diamonds and prosperity. What makes Botswana different? What is the secret?

### Botswana, Rich With Diamonds

Botswana is a diamond-rich country located north of South Africa. Unlike Angola, Sierra Leone, and the Democratic Republic of the Congo, Botswana has had a long tradition of stable democracy, with only three changes in presidency since winning independence in 1966. Botswana's relatively small population of less than 2 million compared to its huge size also plays a role in its political stability. Also, it has strong economic ties with its prosperous neighbor, South Africa, the leading economic power in Southern Africa. Thus, political stability, geographic location, and population demographics contribute to Botswana's economic and political prosperity.

We may conclude, then, that a major factor in whether resources are a blessing or curse is political stability and good governance. Let's turn our attention now to what occupies most people in the African world—agriculture.

## SUBSISTENCE AGRICULTURE

Most Africans depend on subsistence agriculture for their livelihood. They produce their own food by farming small plots and often raise animals, perhaps a few chickens, sheep, goats, or cattle. Many also fish, hunt, or gather. Cash crop agriculture based on cocoa, coffee, peanuts, and rice is also important. Farms are usually small, about 2 to 10 acres (1 to 4 hectares) in size. Mixed cropping, in which different crops are grown together in one plot, is the norm. Maize, peanuts, tomatoes, peppers, and yams may all be planted together in one plot. This lowers the risk of crop failure and guarantees some food security. If one crop fails, another will survive. More important, it supplies all the food needs of the farmer and his immediate family, leaving a little surplus for sale.

### Farming

Subsistence agriculture depends mainly on rainfall. During drought years, crop failures and famine can be widespread. Subsistence farmers are often only one bad harvest away from starvation. During such times, emergency food aid becomes the savior.

After a few years of cultivation, the land is left to rest in order for the soil nutrients to be replenished by natural growth of vegetation. This fallow period can be 10 years or more depending on availability of land. Lately, however, because of increasing population pressure on land, fallow periods of two to three years are quite common. As a result, poor soil fertility and low yields are becoming a major problem. Chemical fertilizers are being used more commonly.

Access to land remains a major challenge for agriculture. Because land belongs to the living, the dead, and those yet to be born, outright sale of land is rare in traditional African society.

A traditional herbal practitioner displays her wares. Rural residents use traditional herbal remedies widely due to the high cost and scarcity of modern biomedical health facilities. Traditional medicines are comprised of mostly roots, tubers, seeds, and tree bark.

The land is passed to heirs, either matrilineally or patrilineally. With time, increasing subdivision among family members has led to land fragmentation. Farmers have increasingly smaller plots of land. Often, such land is not enough to support the

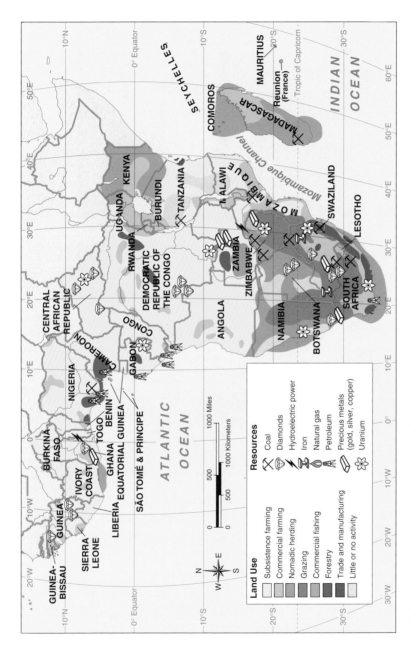

Subsistence farming dominates the land use of the region. This term describes people farming their own food, but having little left over for sale. Africa south of the Sahara is also rich in natural resources.

farmer and his family. Let's check this out in Rwanda, the country with Africa's highest population density.

In the southern province of Gikongoro, Rwanda, we meet Yohanna Nkuliye. He is planting potatoes on a tiny plot of land. Hundreds of tiny plots like his stretch along the valley. Yohanna's father farmed this same land. When he died, it was divided between Yohanna and his four brothers. Yohanna has six sons who have a claim on his farm. "There are more people now and the soil is old. That's why we die of hunger. The land is not enough for my family," he says. Without farmland, many young people leave the rural area to seek opportunities in urban areas. Rwanda has more people per square mile than any other African country, and its increasing rural population is farming progressively smaller parcels of land.

## Raising Cattle

Raising cattle is the dominant activity among the Fulani in northern West Africa and the Masai in East Africa. Their livelihood centers on their cattle. As nomadic peoples, they move with their cattle to find fresh pasture. In Côte d'Ivoire and Nigeria, conflict between cattle herders and crop farmers has intensified as grazing lands have dwindled. In Arusha, Tanzania, tensions between the Asian farmers and local cattle herders recently broke out in violence. Local tribes, mainly migratory cattle herders, had been complaining about the commercial farms that have reduced grazing areas. During dry weather, cattle herders migrate in search of pasture, inevitably bringing them into conflict with the farm owners. Sometimes, severe drought kills tens of thousands of cattle, resulting in extreme hardship for the herders.

## AFRICAN EXPORTS TO THE WORLD

Most African export economies depend on one or two raw materials. Southern Africa exports a wide variety of minerals including gold, diamonds, and platinum. West Africa produces half of the world's cocoa, primarily in Côte d'Ivoire, the world's leading producer, and Ghana. Nigeria is the world's seventh-leading supplier of oil. East African exports tend to be mainly agricultural products, including soybeans and palm oil.

Commercial agriculture for export is becoming increasingly important. The products include cocoa, coffee, tea, rice, palm oil, cotton, peanuts, and maize (corn). Poultry and dairy products are produced for local consumption. Recently, vegetables and cut flowers for export have become important in Kenya, Zimbabwe, and several other countries. Ghana also exports pineapples.

Nevertheless, Africans remain poor because they import more than they export. Also, the prices of their exports fluctuate widely based on supply and demand. In contrast, prices of their imports—petroleum products, machinery, fertilizer, and pharmaceutical products—have either increased or remained fixed. As suppliers of cheap raw materials and low-cost labor, African countries have no control over market prices. Escalating oil prices have forced many governments into debt. Corruption and mismanagement have also retarded economic growth. Sometimes bad national policies contribute to the problems. No country illustrates this better than Zimbabwe.

## ECONOMY AND GOVERNANCE

In Zimbabwe, the government's four-year land redistribution program to undo "colonial wrongs" by giving white-owned land to black Zimbabweans has led to violence, death, and starvation. Land that belonged to white farmers has been confiscated without compensation, and those who resist have been killed. What once were huge commercial farms have been reduced to many small farms. Maize is still planted but only in a small fraction of what used to be and what Zimbabwe needs to feed its population.

The black farm workers whose livelihoods depended on the commercial farms are now suffering. They have no jobs. In a country that used to export maize, charity-feeding programs

Due to the high cost of imported gasoline, shortages are quite common in African countries that don't produce petroleum. In Nigeria, Africa's leading producer and exporter of crude oil, due to corruption and inefficiency, gasoline shortages have become a regular feature. Gasoline queues several miles long choke the narrow roads. A booming black market exists for gasoline, where prices are many times the official fixed prices. This photo shows part of the gasoline queue in Kano in 2003.

feed those who are desperately short of food. Various aid agencies say that children are dying from starvation; some are too weak to walk to get food. Government-controlled television, however, shows happy Zimbabweans reaping record harvests, and the government boasts that there is more maize than the country needs. News reports claim that the government has been using food aid as a political weapon: Those who vote for opposition parties are denied food aid. The land distribution system also favors Mugabe's political allies and friends.

For many Zimbabweans, life has a single constant: waiting in lines. Food is scarce. Gasoline, on the irregular occasions when it is available, sells out quickly. Minibuses, which run along prearranged routes and are the most important public transportation, are few and the lines for them are long. Seven in 10 Zimbabweans are officially out of work and do whatever they can to survive. The food shortages are even more punishing in rural areas, worsened by the drought that hit southern Africa last year.

Rampant inflation means that fat piles of banknotes are often needed for simple transactions. The Zimbabwean dollar is in freefall. The official rate is 825 to the U.S. dollar, but the black market rate is more than 5,000. Foreign currency is in short supply because of lack of exports.

According to President Robert Mugabe, Zimbabwe's ruler since independence in 1980, the economy is under attack, sabotaged by Great Britain and its allies. This is revenge for Mugabe's policy of redistributing land from white farmers to the majority black population. Independent economists say that it is because the land reform and general economy have been grossly mismanaged. Many of the farms confiscated remain fallow, without cultivation.

Many African leaders are on Mugabe's side. They see this as a postcolonial issue in which Great Britain is penalizing Zimbabwe for having the audacity to take land from white owners. Unfortunately, that support does not help Zimbabweans improve their circumstances. For the moment, then, the lines are likely to keep getting longer.

## AFRICA'S INADEQUATE INFRASTRUCTURE

Poor infrastructure—highways, railroads, and communication facilities—poses a major problem that hinders the African world's economic growth. Good roads are few and congested. Rail connections are limited except in Southern and East Africa. In many countries, food production areas are linked only by dirt roads that become impassable during the rainy season. Improvements in the transportation network are desperately needed. Because of poor roads, automobile accidents are frequent and a leading cause of death.

There are some encouraging signs. Various links of the Pan-African Highway system have gradually fallen into place. The trans-Saharan route in Northern Africa is expected to link to the West African road network and the Trans-East African Highway. When the improvements on these major highways are completed, it will be possible to travel from Algiers on the Mediterranean Sea to Mombasa on the Indian Ocean and then to Dakar on the Atlantic Ocean and from Cairo to Gaborone in Botswana.

The Internet finally is making its way into the remote African villages. Communications centers, where people can surf the Internet and send e-mails, are expanding. The numerous e-mails from Africa that invite unsuspecting Americans to "provide a bank account number to permit the transfer of millions of dollars to you for a fee" confirm the widespread Internet access.

Already, new technologies are making an impact in democratic expression. True participatory democracy is emerging, with the numerous talk shows on which citizens contribute to national debate. Ghana's media are playing a vital role in the country's evolving democracy. From only four state-controlled newspapers and the Ghana Broadcasting Corporation (with its radio and television divisions) in 1990, the media have expanded to 127 radio stations, 6 television stations, and more than 60 newspapers. Recently, Ghana's president was quoted as saying, "Now there is freedom everywhere and people are not afraid to express their views and even insult the president. This is the price we have to pay for democracy and it is good." In the 2000 elections, many radio stations sent correspondents to voting places; acts of intimidation and attempted vote rigging were reported to the public. The peace Ghana is enjoying in a West Africa under turmoil is partly the result of free media.

Africa remains behind the rest of the world in taking advantage of the communication and information revolutions. Limited and expensive communication infrastructure and lack of skills and awareness are some limiting factors. Cell phones, however, are widely used and seem to be the technology of choice.

A recent story that appeared in the BBC news confirms the popularity of cell phones in Africa. Three men died while trying to retrieve a mobile phone from a pit latrine in the Kenyan town of Mombasa. University student Dora Mwabela dropped the phone into the latrine while she was using the facility. She offered a reward of 1,000 shillings ($13) for anyone who could recover the phone (Most Kenyans survive on less than one dollar per day).

First, recently married radio technician Patrick Luhakha tried to retrieve the phone. He ripped up the toilet floor and climbed down a ladder into the latrine. When nothing was heard from him, a neighbor, Kevin Wambua, went to check on his friend. He slipped and fell into the putrid mess and was unable to get out. A third man, John Solo, tried to rescue the two, while policemen stood and watched. He collapsed while halfway down the ladder. Neighbors managed to carry him to the surface, but he died on the way to a hospital. The cell phone was not found.

## CHALLENGES TO AFRICA'S YOUNG

Two huge problems threaten young people in the African World—war and the prevalence of HIV/AIDS that makes orphans of millions of young people.

### Youngsters and the HIV/AIDS crisis

The most serious problem is the HIV/AIDS crisis. More than 2.5 million Africans die from the disease each year. In Botswana, nearly 40 percent of the population ages 15 to 49 is infected with HIV. Approximately one-third of the population is infected in Lesotho, Swaziland, and Zimbabwe. Not all countries have been affected as severely: In Senegal and Mali, only 1 to 2 percent of the adult population is infected. In fact, more than 90 percent of Africans are HIV free. Keeping them HIV free, however, is a challenge. The tragedy of AIDS is most visible in the lives of AIDS orphans. Ninety-five percent of the world's AIDS orphans live in Africa. Let's meet two of them.

Pepile is seven years old and very ill. Her father and younger brother died of AIDS; her mother is HIV positive. So is Pepile. She is one of millions of Africans who are living with HIV and AIDS. Pepile lives in a bare, stone home at the end of a dusty hillside trail in the rolling countryside of KwaZulu-Natal in South Africa. She is bright and loves to talk, but she knows she is desperately ill. There are no drugs for her, just as there are no drugs for the vast majority of Africans who are living with HIV/AIDS.

Eight-year old Emmanuel Kalunga lives in Zambia and is now the head of the family. His mother Lydia, age 26, is dying of AIDS, which already has killed his father and young brother. Lydia has just a few weeks to live. Her mother, Emmanuel's grandmother, is also sick with AIDS. They are desperately poor and often go for days without food. Emmanuel's job is to care for them both. He is not in school. In northern Zambia, where Emmanuel lives, children grow up fast. One in four has been orphaned by AIDS. Because of the virus, Zambian parents are dying young: Few live beyond the age of 30. Each day, another 500 people are infected with HIV. For orphans with no education and no job prospects, life is difficult. A large number of orphans, like Mable and her twin sisters, Tangu and Nyuma, turn to prostitution. They were abandoned when their parents died. The most tragic aspect of HIV/AIDS is that it kills young adults, parents, teachers, skilled workers, and trained professionals in the prime of their lives.

### Child Soldiers in War

Have you ever dreamed about going to war? Do you fantasize about joining the military and fighting in the War on Terror? Perhaps you have even played war games on the computer and imagined what real war must be like. For many African children, war is not a game, a dream, or a fantasy. War is real.

In many parts of Africa, including Sierra Leone, the Democratic Republic of the Congo, and Sudan, children are abducted or recruited by force to fight in war. Some children join armed groups out of desperation. Having been driven out of their homes and often separated from family members, many children see joining the armed groups as their best chance for survival. Others seek escape from poverty or a chance to avenge family members who have been killed. They all follow orders under threat of death.

Children make obedient soldiers because they are physically vulnerable and easily intimidated by their captors. Human Rights Watch has interviewed child soldiers from Angola, Liberia, Sierra Leone, Sudan, and Uganda. In Sierra Leone, thousands of children abducted by rebel forces witnessed and participated in horrible atrocities against civilians, including beheadings, amputations, rape, and burning people alive. Children forced to take part in atrocities were often given drugs

Girls are also used as soldiers. In addition to combat duties, they are subject to sexual abuse and may be taken as "wives" by rebel leaders. In Northern Uganda, Human Rights Watch interviewed girls who had been impregnated by rebel commanders and then were forced to strap their babies on their backs and take up arms against Ugandan security forces.

Because of their immaturity and lack of experience, child soldiers suffer higher casualties than adults. Even after the conflict is over, they may be left physically disabled or psychologically damaged. Lacking an education or regular job skills, many find it difficult to rejoin peaceful society. Traumatized by war, former child soldiers are often drawn into crime or become easy prey for future recruitment. Let's meet some child soldiers from Liberia.

Fourteen-year-old David Smith dropped out of primary school and picked up a gun in 1999, when he was only nine years old. After his parents were killed in his presence, he joined the rebel army to avoid being killed. Now, he does not want to be reminded of war any more. He wants to go to school and learn a trade to get a good job.

Sixteen-year-old Marilyn Taylor spent three years fighting for the Liberians United for Reconciliation and Democracy (LURD) rebel group. She dropped out of school in the fourth grade because her parents could not afford it. Her parents were killed in the war. She doesn't like to talk about her experiences in war but admits she was raped numerous times by her commanders. Now all she wants is to go to school, but most of the schools outside Monrovia, the capital, are still in ruins and private schools still demand high fees.

Life in the African world is not easy, especially for children. Despite massive natural resources, poverty, disease, and war make life very difficult. What is the future like for the African world and its children? We will examine this in the next chapter.

# Future of the African World

O n the basis of what most Americans see in the media, the African world's future seems grim. Armed children fighting in brutal wars, AIDS deaths and orphans, and widespread political chaos are regular media fare. This is not the everyday reality for the majority of Africans. Most people enjoy ordinary daily life as we know it. Children go to school, play, and walk in the park free of danger and violence. In most countries, people are not starving; they are well fed and content. They may not have electricity or computers, but they are happy. They are not dying of AIDS. Starvation is present but usually only in war-torn or drought-prone areas such as Ethiopia.

What is the future of the African world? This question is addressed by focusing on four regions: West Africa, Central Africa, East

Africa, and Southern Africa. In each region, case studies will focus on success, problems, and failure.

## WEST AFRICA
### The Fall of Côte d'Ivoire
Once hailed as a model of political and economic stability and religious and ethnic harmony, Côte d'Ivoire is now plagued by internal strife. Civil war that began in 2002 left the country divided between the rebel-held north and army-controlled south. Peacekeepers patrol the buffer zone that separates the areas. Political efforts to reunite the nation have failed so far. Elections are planned for 2005, but there are other problems. About 10 percent of the adult population is living with HIV. Unless the political conflict is resolved quickly, the prosperity and stability will melt away. For Côte d'Ivoire, the future is quite uncertain.

### Nigeria: Tottering Giant
After years of revolving-door military coups, Nigeria now has elected leadership. Still, ethnic and religious conflicts threaten to break apart Africa's most populous country. Since return to civilian rule in 1999, militants from religious and ethnic groups have expressed their frustrations more freely and with increasing violence in the name of political freedom. Thousands of people have already died in ethnic violence, and separatist aspirations among some groups have been growing.

Islamic law (sharia) imposed in several northern states has worsened relations and caused thousands of Christians to flee. The government is under pressure to improve the economy, which experienced an oil boom in the 1970s. Much of the potential wealth has been lost as a result of widespread government corruption and mismanagement. Nigeria is the world's seventh-largest oil producer, and it seeks to attract foreign investment. Security concerns (possible terrorist cells in northern Nigeria) and poor infrastructure, particularly incessant power cuts, are obstacles. Nigeria's future depends on the government's ability to control ethnic violence and the burgeoning crime problem. Keeping the 120 million people together in one Nigeria remains a difficult challenge.

## Ghana: Struggling to Stand

Ghana, the first African country to gain independence, was also the first to experience military coups and the first to adopt IMF- and World Bank-imposed structural adjustment. Since April 1992, when a constitution that allows for a multiparty system was approved in a referendum, Ghana has been on a stable path toward economic stability and democracy. It has largely escaped the civil strife that plagues other West African countries.

Today, Ghana is an island of political and economic stability in West Africa. After peaceful elections in 2004, Ghana seems to be well on its way to a bright future. Many Ghanaians who left their country during political and economic hard times are beginning to return home. For Ghana, the future is bright. Kwame Nkrumah's Black Star appears poised to shine once again.

## EAST AFRICA

East Africa is a troubled region. The northern part is particularly volatile. Because of conflicts among countries, the prospect of regional economic integration is slim. Refugees fleeing armed conflict are everywhere. Each country harbors refugees as well as dissidents from neighboring countries. Frequent droughts compound the effects of these conflicts. The southern part of East Africa is relatively more stable, but even there relations are strained by ideological differences. Relations between Kenya and Tanzania deteriorated to the point that their common border was closed for many years. Similarly, relations between Uganda and Kenya have been strained by claims that each has harbored the other's dissidents. Let's look closely at Somalia, Kenya, and Tanzania.

## Somalia: Turmoil and Chaos

After President Mohamed Siad Barre was overthrown in 1991, Somalia had no effective central government for much of the remaining decade. Famine, fighting among rival warlords, and disease killed up to one million people. A transitional government that was set up in 2000 to reconcile warring militias only controls parts of the capital. Ongoing territorial claims on Somali-inhabited areas of Ethiopia, Kenya, and Djibouti mean more conflict. Self-proclaimed states of Somaliland and Puntland run their own affairs. In 2004, after protracted talks in Kenya, the main warlords and politicians signed a deal to set up a new parliament, which would appoint a new president. National reconciliation talks have been plagued by delays and boycotts. For Somalia, the future is quite dismal. The state may fracture even further. The new government remains in exile in Kenya, waiting to go home.

## Kenya: Overcoming Corruption and Terrorism

Kenya's ethnic diversity has produced a vibrant culture but is also a source of conflict. With its scenic beauty and abundant wildlife, Kenya is one of Africa's major safari destinations, but the lucrative tourist industry has been hit by fears of terrorism. Flight cancellations and travel warnings issued by some foreign governments have had a severe impact on tourism. Corruption is a major problem. Key donors, including the World Bank, withheld much-needed aid because of uncontrolled corruption under Daniel arap Moi, who remained in power for 24 years. President Mwai Kibaki has pledged to tackle the problem.

Other pressing challenges include high unemployment, crime, and poverty. Most Kenyans live below the poverty level of one dollar per day. One of Africa's more politically stable countries, Kenya has been a leading light in the Somali and Sudanese peace processes. For Kenya, like Ghana, the future is quite bright, unless a major terrorist attack occurs in the country.

## Tanzania: From Socialism to Capitalism

Tanzania lacks the internal strife that is present in many African countries. Still, it remains one of the world's poorest countries, heavily reliant on foreign aid and with many of its people living below the poverty line. Tanzania has few exportable minerals and a primitive agricultural system. In 1967, its first president, Julius Nyerere, embarked on African socialism, which called for self-reliance through cooperative farm villages and the nationalization of factories, plantations, banks, and private companies.

Ten years later, the program had completely failed because of inefficiency, corruption, resistance from farmers, and the rise in price of imported petroleum. Tanzania's economic woes were compounded in 1979 and 1981 by a costly military intervention to overthrow President Idi Amin of Uganda.

To improve the economy, the government is trying to attract foreign investment and loans by dismantling government control of the economy. Depending on how successful these efforts are, Tanzanians could see an improvement in quality of life. The stable government is a plus.

## CENTRAL AFRICA
## Rwanda: Beyond Ethnic Cleansing

Rwanda is still recovering from the shock of Africa's worst genocide in modern times. Intervention in the conflict in the neighboring Democratic Republic of the Congo has marred recovery efforts. Ethnic tension between the dominant Tutsi minority and the majority Hutu resulted in the massacre of an estimated 800,000 people, mostly Tutsi. Three million Hutu refugees fled to neighboring countries. Among them were the perpetrators of the genocide, who turned into a rebel force that menaces Rwanda's borders.

The government has made significant efforts to promote unity among Tutsi and Hutu. It has abolished those ethnic labels in favor of a single Rwandan identity. Still, ethnicity is a potentially divisive issue. Perceptions that Tutsi occupy the most important positions in the army and the civil administration and have the most important posts in the economy remain. There are fears that a sense of political and economic exclusion will lead to growing resentment among Hutu. How the government responds to demands for greater political freedom and more equitably shared economic opportunities will determine how long Rwanda's current stability lasts.

## Gabon: Forced Stability

Political stability and oil have given Gabon the highest income per capita in Central and Western Africa. Since winning independence from France in 1960, Gabon has had just two presidents, the current having been in power since 1967. Although home to more than 40 ethnic groups, Gabon has escaped the strife that afflicts other West African states. This can be attributed to its relative prosperity and to the continued presence of French troops.

Gabon's heavy dependence on oil means that fluctuations in oil prices have a very severe effect. When oil prices began to fall in the late 1980s, opposition to the president increased, culminating in demonstrations in 1990. These ushered in political liberalization, and, in 1991, a new constitution that instituted a multiparty system was adopted. In short, as long as the oil flows and the good times roll, Gabon has a bright and stable future. Will the oil last forever?

## Democratic Republic of the Congo: Fighting for Diamonds

A vast country with immense economic resources, the Democratic Republic of Congo has been at the center of what could be termed Africa's "world war." The five-year war claimed an estimated 3 million lives, either as a direct result of fighting or because of disease, malnutrition, and starvation. Government forces supported by Angola, Namibia, and Zimbabwe fought against rebels backed by Uganda and Rwanda. Fighting was fuelled by the country's vast mineral wealth, with all sides taking advantage of the anarchy to plunder the DRC's natural resources, particularly diamonds.

A peace deal was reached, and a transitional government was established in 2003. Former rebels have joined a power-sharing government, and planned general elections may bring some stability. Nonetheless, troubles are not completely over. The government has no control over large parts of the country. The success of ongoing peacekeeping efforts and an end to conflict will determine the future of this potentially great country.

## SOUTHERN AFRICA
### Botswana: Diamonds and HIV/AIDS

Botswana is Africa's longest continuous multiparty democracy and perhaps the continent's most stable country. It is relatively free of corruption and has a good human rights record. Botswana is also the world's leading diamond producer and protects some of the continent's largest areas of wilderness. The country is sparsely populated because it is so dry. The Kalahari Desert, home to the dwindling group of Bushman hunters and gatherers, makes up much of the country, and most areas are too arid to sustain any agriculture other than cattle grazing.

Despite its economic success, Botswana has an enormous problem. It has the highest incidence of AIDS in Africa. Foreign investment has led to better transportation links, which in turn have aided the spread of HIV/AIDS. The disease has left many thousands of children orphaned and has dramatically reduced the life expectancy rate. More than one in three adults in Botswana are believed to be living with HIV. Despite the HIV epidemic, Botswana still has a promising future. Medication that can help stabilize AIDS patients is becoming available in the country.

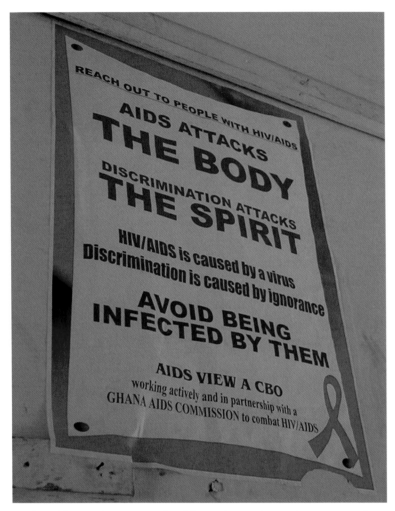

HIV/AIDS is a major concern in Africa today. In December 2004, Africa had 10 percent of the world's population, but 70 percent of the HIV/AIDS cases, 80 percent of the AIDS deaths, and 90 percent of the AIDS orphans. South Africa had the world's highest number of people living with AIDS.

### Zimbabwe: Land Reform, Repression, and Starvation

Zimbabwe is home to the Victoria Falls, one of world's natural wonders. It is also the site of the stone enclosures of Great Zimbabwe, remnants of a past empire, and to herds of elephants and other big game animals that roam vast stretches of wilderness. Zimbabwe faces major political and social strife, as well as an economy in shambles. For years it has been a leading producer of tobacco and a breadbasket for surrounding countries that often depend on food imports. The seizure of almost all white-owned commercial agricultural land, with the stated aim of benefiting black farmers, led to a sharp decline in crop production. By 2003, millions of Zimbabweans were thought to be at risk of famine. The country's current challenges include the need to address the political stalemate, the economic crisis, and one of the world's highest rates of HIV/AIDS infection. The future of the country depends on how quickly President Mugabe hands over power and allows democracy to function. Until then, Zimbabwe faces chaos and doom.

## South Africa: Rich Rainbow Nation Faces HIV and Crime

Diversity characterizes South Africa. It is a country with 11 official languages. Community leaders include rabbis and chieftains. Traditional healers ply their trades around the corner from stockbrokers, and housing ranges from mud huts to palatial homes with swimming pools. South Africa is indeed a rainbow nation. Most of these diverse communities, however, have not had much representation for long.

Until 1994, a white minority ruled South Africa with an iron fist. Under the leadership of Nelson Mandela and other activists, apartheid finally ended and democracy was extended to the rest of South Africa's people. The white government had separated the races and resettled hundreds of thousands of people by force. They poisoned and bombed opponents and encouraged trouble in neighboring countries. The apartheid government eventually negotiated itself out of power, and the new leadership encouraged reconciliation. The lingering costs of past racial conflict will be paid for years to come in the form of lawlessness, social disruption, and lost education.

South Africa is a regional economic giant. The strong economy built on communications, energy, transportation, mining, and political stability makes the country resilient. Major problems facing the country include HIV/AIDS, serious crime, and widespread poverty that results from years of officially enforced inequity. Despite these problems, South Africa has a bright future.

## CONCLUSION

Africa's poverty and political instability can be traced directly to its history, especially to colonialism. Colonialism took control of Africa and its many resources away from Africans. Today, outsiders continue to control and devour Africa's resources. The artificial political boundaries and alien political systems imposed on Africans continue to produce tremors of war and instability.

Africans are beginning to struggle with African solutions to their problems. They can not surmount their problems alone, however. They need assistance from the countries that were responsible for the region's present-day predicament and that benefited from its wealth. Perhaps Africa's debt to foreign governments can be cancelled or reduced. This would allow money that would have been spent on debt reduction to be directed toward improving education, health care, and other critical services. Perhaps the rich countries of the world can lower tariffs on African manufactured goods to encourage African industrial development and production. That way, we can trade with them, not just give them aid. The United States has a fine example of what could be done: the African Growth and Opportunities Act (AGOA). Under this, African countries export textile products to the United States without any tariffs. Can this be expanded to cover other products? Could other countries follow the American example?

African states now realize that, as individual countries divided by artificial borders imposed by outsiders, they can be exploited and manipulated too easily. In fact, many African leaders now recognize that, without cooperation, their countries can not survive. This is why they have created the African Union. A new economic bloc that includes South Africa and many other African states will be more sustainable than would individual countries negotiating with the European Union or NAFTA.

Good governance is critical. African leaders have to begin to look beyond "My Own Interest," as Kenyans translated the letters in the name of corrupt ex-President arap Moi, to long-term national and African interests. They are off to a good start with the signing of the NEPAD agreement. Under this program, African countries will be evaluated in regard to critical matters such as effective government and corruption. Ghana has volunteered to be the first country for the peer review. Hopefully, other countries will follow and good governance and political freedom will spread throughout the African world.

Perhaps the many crises of the African world have accomplished one important thing—driving African countries towards unity. An African Union is an idea long overdue. To promote economic growth, Africans need to unite against HIV, poverty, and bad government. A united Africa could become a major economic power. Until then many African children wait, and pray, for food and peace while numerous others live normal lives.

| Country | Land Area (sq mi) | Population 2004 in Millions |
|---|---|---|
| Angola | 481,351 | 13.4 |
| Central African Republic | 340,533 | 3.7 |
| Congo | 132,046 | 3.4 |
| Democratic Republic of the Congo | 905,531 | 58.7 |
| Gabon | 103,347 | 1.2 |
| Burundi | 10,745 | 7.0 |
| Kenya | 224,081 | 32.4 |
| Rwanda | 10,170 | 7.7 |
| Uganda | 93,066 | 26.2 |
| United Republic of Tanzania | 394,900 | 39.2 |
| Benin | 43,483 | 7.0 |
| Cameroon | 183,568 | 17.0 |
| Cape Verde | 1,556 | 0.5 |
| Côte d'Ivoire | 124,502 | 16.8 |
| Equatorial Guinea | 10,830 | 0.5 |
| Gambia | 4,363 | 1.6 |
| Ghana | 92,100 | 21.1 |
| Guinea | 94,927 | 8.9 |
| Guinea-Bissau | 13,946 | 1.4 |
| Liberia | 43,000 | 3.5 |
| Nigeria | 356,668 | 129.0 |
| Sao Tome and Principe | 371 | 0.2 |
| Senegal | 75,954 | 10.4 |
| Sierra Leone | 27,699 | 5.9 |
| Togo | 21,927 | 5.6 |
| Botswana | 224,606 | 1.6 |
| Lesotho | 11,718 | 2.3 |
| Madagascar | 226,656 | 17.6 |
| Malawi | 45,745 | 11.4 |
| Mozambique | 309,494 | 20.4 |
| Namibia | 318,259 | 1.9 |
| South Africa | 471,444 | 44.5 |
| Swaziland | 6,703 | 1.1 |
| Zambia | 290,583 | 10.4 |
| Zimbabwe | 105,873 | 12.5 |
| Burkina Faso | 105,792 | 13.4 |
| Mali | 478,838 | 12.0 |
| Niger | 489,189 | 12.4 |
| TOTAL | 6,875,564 | 584 |

109

| 2–3 million years ago | Evidence shows early humans in Africa. |
|---|---|
| 130,000 years ago | Humans leave Africa to populate the Old World. |

## Pre-colonization

| 200 B.C. | The Nok culture is at its height. |
|---|---|
| 100 B.C. | Bantu people introduce iron working into the area south of the Sudan. |
| A.D. 1 | East African city-states begin. |
| 100 | Bantu migration begins. |

## 400–1500 Kingdoms and Empires

| 300–700 | The Kingdom of Axum is in power. |
|---|---|
| 900 | Sudanese kingdoms begin. |
| 900–1100 | The Kingdom of Ghana is in power. |
| 1200 | Hausa city-states begin. |
| 1200–1450 | The Kingdom of Mali is in power. |
| 900s–1400s | Great Zimbabwe is in power. |
| 1450 | Oyo Empire is founded. |
| 1460–1591 | Songhai Empire is in power. |

## 1400–1950 European Exploration and Colonization of Africa

| 1444–1445 | Portuguese make contact with Sub-Saharan Africa. |
|---|---|
| 1471 | Portuguese arrive in the Gold Coast. |
| 1479 | Portuguese build Elmina Castle on West African Coast. |
| 1482 | Portuguese begin building Elmina Castle on the Gold Coast. |
| 1488 | Bartholomew Diaz goes around the Cape of Good Hope. |
| 1490 | First Portuguese missionaries go to Congo. |
| 1652 | Dutch establish colony at Cape of Good Hope, South Africa. |

## The Atlantic Slave Trade

**1497** Vasco da Gama [Portuguese] sails to East Africa.

**1510** First slaves are shipped to Spanish colonies in South America via Spain.

**1518** First direct shipment of slaves goes from Africa to the Americas.

**1780s** Slave trade is at its peak.

**1807** British abolish slave trade.

**1808** Sierra Leone is declared a colony.

**1814** The Dutch outlaw slave trade.

**1816** Gambia is occupied by the British.

**1820** British settlers land on Eastern Cape.

**1822** Liberia colony is established by returning former slaves.

**1834** British law is passed declaring ownership of slaves illegal.

**1847** Liberia declares independence.

**1848** Slavery is abolished throughout the French Empire.

**1865** 13th Amendment abolishes slavery in the United States of America.

**1869** Portugal abolishes slavery.

**1867** First diamonds are found in Hopetown, Cape Colony, South Africa.

**1869** The Suez Canal is completed.

**1872** Cape Colony is made self-governing.


## Pre-independence

**1884–1885** The Berlin Conference partitions Africa among the European powers.

**1885** First telegraph cable is laid between West Africa and Europe.

**1896** Asantehene (king of Asanti) is forced into exile by the British.

**1912** ANC is established as South African Native Congress.

**1914–1918** World War I takes place.

**1920** The National Congress of British West Africa is established with branches in Sierra Leone, Gambia, Nigeria and the Gold Coast, calling for elected element in territorial legislature.

**1922** Egypt gains independence.

**1925** West African Students' Union is founded in London.

**1935** Italy invades Abyssinia (Ethiopia).

**1936** Emperor Haile Selassie goes into exile.

**1939** World War II begins.

**1941** Emperor Haile Selassie returns to Ethiopia.

**1942** West Africans Burma campaign.

**1944** Kenya Africa Union established; syndicat Agricole Africain formed in Ivory Coast by Felix Houphouet-Boigny.

## 1950–present Decolonization and Independence

**1948** First apartheid legislation passes in South Africa.

**1957** Ghana becomes the first independent African nation.

**1958** All-African People's Conference convenes in Accra.

**1960** Congo is granted independence from Belgium.

**1962** Algeria gains independence from France.

**1963** Organization for African Unity is formed.

## Independence

**Before WW2** Ethiopia, Liberia, Egypt.

**1950s** Libya, Sudan, Morocco, Tunisia, Ghana, Guinea.

**1960** Cameroon, Togo, Senegal, Mali, Madagascar, Zaire, Somalia, Benin, Niger, Burkina Faso (originally Upper Volta/Haute Volta), Cote D'Ivoire (Ivory Coast), Chad, Central African Republic, Congo (Brazzaville), Gabon, Nigeria, Mauritania.

**1961** Tanzania, Sierra Leone.

**1962** Burundi, Rwanda, Algeria, Uganda.

**1962** Nelson Mandela is arrested and sentenced to life imprisonment for plotting to overthrow the South African government.

**1963** Zanzibar (union with Tanganyika 1964), Kenya.

**1964** Malawi, Zambia (formerly Northern Rhodesia).

| | |
|---|---|
| **1965** | Gambia. |
| **1966** | Botswana, Lesotho. |
| **1968** | Mauritius, Swaziland, Equatorial Guinea. |
| **1974** | Guinea Bissau. |
| **1975** | Mozambique, Cape Verde, Comoros, Sao Tome and Principe, Angola, Western Sahara. |
| **1976** | Seychelles. |
| **1977** | Djibouti. |
| **1980** | Zimbabwe (formerly Southern Rhodesia). |
| **1990** | Namibia (formerly South West Africa). |
| **1990** | Nelson Mandela is freed after 27 years as a political prisoner. |
| **1991–1993** | Apartheid is abolished. |

## Present Era

| | |
|---|---|
| **1981** | World Bank and International Monetary Fund begin imposing Structural Adjustment Programs. |
| **1994** | South Africa's first multiracial democratic elections are held; Nelson Mandela becomes first president of multiracial South Africa, under Black majority rule. |
| **1994** | About one million people, mostly Tutsis are massacred in the 100-day Hutu-Tutsi Massacre. About 3 million Hutu refugees flee to neighboring countries. |
| **2000** | The New Economic Partnership for Africa's Development (NEPAD) is formed. African leaders promise to deliver good governance, peace, and security in exchange for increased foreign investment. |
| **2001** | OAU becomes the African Union, loosely modeled after the European Union. |

## BOOKS

Aryeetey-Attoh, S., ed. *Geography of Sub-Saharan Africa.* 2d ed. Upper Saddle River, NJ: Pearson Education, Inc., 2003.

Domingo, V. *South Africa.* Philadelphia: Chelsea House Publishers, 2004.

Gritzner, J. *Senegal.* Philadelphia: Chelsea House Publishers, 2005.

Kalipeni, E., S. Craddock, J. R. Oppong, and J. Ghosh. *HIV & AIDS in Africa: Beyond Epidemiology.* Oxford, UK: Blackwell Publishing, 2004.

Oppong, J. R., and E. D. Oppong. *Kenya.* Philadelphia: Chelsea House Publishers, 2004.

Oppong, J. R., and E. D. Oppong. *Ghana.* Philadelphia: Chelsea House Publishers, 2003.

Phillips, D. *Nigeria.* Philadelphia: Chelsea House Publishers, 2004.

Russell, R. J., F. B. Kniffen, and E. L. Pruitt. *Culture Worlds.* New York: Macmillan, 1969.

Stock, R. *Africa South of the Sahara: A Geographical Interpretation.* 2d ed. New York: Guilford, 2004.

## WEBSITES

African Food - History for Kids
http://www.historyforkids.org/**learn**/**africa**/food/

Africa for Kids
http://www.pbs.org/wnet/africa/

African News
http://allafrica.com/

British Broadcasting Corporation — African Country Profiles
http://news.bbc.co.uk/2/hi/africa/country_profiles/

Central Intelligence Agency. CIA World Fact Book 2004 — African countries
http://www.cia.gov/cia/publications/factbook/

The Library of Congress Country Studies
http://lcweb2.loc.gov/frd/cs/cshome.html

Peace Corps Kids World—South Africa
http://www.peacecorps.gov/kids/world/africa/southafrica.html

PBS Kids' Africa
http://www.pbs.org/wonders/Kids/cloth/cloth.htm

Abacha, Sani, 11
Aburi Botanical Garden, 24
Adornment, 61–62
African Anglican Church, 59
African Growth and Opportunities
    Act (AGOA), 107
African Union, 71
Aging, 64
Agriculture
    cattle in, 89
    children in, 44–45
    commercial, 90
    farming in, early, 29
    land access in, 86–89
    origins of, 30
    rain-fed, 9, 86
    subsistence, 86–89
AIDS. See HIV/AIDS
Air mass, 20
Akan, 4
    aging and, 64
    dress of, 61
    family size in, 43–44
    political system of, 62
    religion of, 56
    social values of, 62
Alhaji, 58
Allah, 58
al Qaeda, 12–13
Amin, Idi, 11, 102
Anglican Church, 59
Angola
    child soldiers in, 96
    diamonds and conflict in, 85
    independence of, 40
    oil in, 83
Animism, traditional, 56–58
Annan, Kofi, 6
Apartheid, 6
Archaeologists, 28
Arusha, 89
Assimilation, 36
Atlas Mountains, 15
Axum culture, 30
Azikiwe, Nnamdi, 38

Banda, Hastings Kamuzu, 72
Banjul, 16
Barre, Mohamed Siad, 101
Barter, 31
Bauxite, 84
Berlin Conference of 1884–1885, 35
Biafran War, 75
Bin Laden, Osama, 12–13
Birthplace of humanity, 1, 28
Botanical gardens, 24
Botswana
    diamonds in, 84–86, 104
    economic growth in, 2
    HIV/AIDS in, 6, 94–95, 104
    life expectancy and infant mortality
        in, 46
    political stability of, 85
Breakaway movements, 74
Buses. See Minibuses (taxi)
Bushman, 104

Camel trade, 31
Cape Range, 15
Cape Town, commuting in, 53–54
Cattle, raising, 89
Cell phones, 94
Central Africa, 102–104
Cherubim, 59
Children
    as labor force, 43–44
    life of, 47
    as soldiers, 96–97
    treasuring of, 63–64
Christianity, 58–59
    spread of, 34, 38
Chromium, 84
Cities, primate, 48
Climate, 18–21
Climate change, 25–27
Coastlines, 16
Cocoa export, 89–90
Cocoa production
    in Côte d'Ivoire, 67, 89–90
    in Ghana, 73
Colonialism, impact of, 36–38

Colonial rule, 35–36
Commerce, centers of, 30–31
Communication facilities, 93, 94
Commuting, in Cape Town, 53–54
Complementarity, 30
Conflict
    culture and, 66–68
    diamonds and, 84–85
    religion and, 61
Congo River, 17
Continentality, 20–21
Continental shelf, 16
Continental tropical air mass, 20
Convention People's Party, 38–39
Copper, 84
Côte d'Ivoire, 4–6
    cocoa production in, 67, 89–90
    ethnic conflict in, 67–68
    fall of, 99
    HIV/AIDS in, 99
    politics in, 71
Countries. *See also* specific countries
    in Africa, 7, 109
Coups, military, 72, 74
    in Ghana, 73–74
Cradle of humanity, 1, 28
Cultural diffusion, 29
Cultural diversity, 8–9
Culture and society, 55–68
    adornment and symbolism in,
        61–62
    beginnings of, 1
    conflict and, 66–68
    family in, 62–65
    funerals in (*See* Funerals)
    marriage in, 66
    names in, 65–66
    religion in, 56–61
        (*See also* Religion)
Culture hearths, early, 29–30
Culture region, 6–8
Currency, for early trade, 31
Cyclones, 27

Dairy products, 90
Dancing, 60

Dar es Salaam, 48
Darfur conflict, 66–67
Date palm, 21
Democratic Republic of the Congo,
        103–104
    after independence, 74–75
    child soldiers in, 96
    conflict in, 77
    diamonds in, 103–104
    ethnic groups in, 9
    natural resources of, 84
Department of Homeland Security,
        12
Desert, 3, 21
    population in, 43
Development, 82–86
Diamonds, 84–86
    in Botswana, 84, 85–86
    conflict and, 84–85
    in Democratic Republic of the
        Congo, 103–104
    mining of, 2, 10
    in Sierra Leone, 84–85
Disease, 12
Dissent, political, 71
Dividing Africa, Europeans in, 34–35
Dress, 61–62
Drought, 9

East Africa, 100–102
Economic development policies, 75–76
Economy, 81–97
    in Botswana, 2
    child soldiers and, 96–97
    exports in, 89–90
    governance and, 90–92
    HIV/AIDS in young and, 94–95
    infrastructure on, 92–94
    natural resources, development,
        and poverty in, 82–86
    subsistence agriculture in, 86–89
    youth challenges in, 94–97
Ecotourism, 22
Elephant poaching, 25
Employment, lack of, 49

Environmental problems, 23–27. *See also* Environmental problems
  climate change in, 25–27
  declining wildlife in, 25
  dwindling forests in, 23–25
  weather and food security in, 27
Equator, 3, 20
Eritrea, 75
Ethiopia
  Eritrean resistance in, 75
  highlands of, 23
  poverty in, 9
Ethiopian Orthodox Church, 58–59
Ethnic conflict
  in Côte d'Ivoire, 67–68
  in Darfur, 66–67
  in Nigeria, 67
  in Rwanda, 102–103
Ethnic groups, 8–9
  in Democratic Republic of the
    Congo, 9
European colonial rule, 35–36
European contact, 31–34
  dividing Africa in, 34–35
  silent trade in, 31–32
  slave trade in, 32–34
European domination, 8
Exploitation
  direct, 36
  European, 35–36
Exports, to world, 89–90

Family, 62–65
Family size, 45
Farming. *See also* Agriculture
  early, 29
  subsistence, 9, 86–89
Fertility rate, 44–45
Fishing and fisheries, 16, 26–27
Flooding, 27
Flower exports, 90
Food aid, as political weapon, 91
Food security, weather and, 27
Food shortages, in Zimbabwe, 92
Forests, dwindling, 23–25

Freetown, 16
Fulani, 37, 89
Funerals, 9–10
  cost of, 65
  dancing at, 60
Future, 98–108
  of Central Africa, 102–104
  conclusion on, 107–108
  of East Africa, 100–102
  of southern Africa, 104–107
  of West Africa, 99–100

Gabon, 103
  oil in, 13, 103
Gambia, land area of, 3, 109
Game, 22
Gardens, botanical, 24
Gasoline shortages, 91
Geographic location, 3. *See also*
  specific locations
Geography
  historical, 28–40 (*See also*
    Historical geography)
  physical, 14–27 (*See also* Physical
    geography)
Ghana
  cocoa production in, 73
  future of, 99–100
  gold mining in, 2
  independence struggle in, 38–39
  life in, 4–6
  media in, 93
  NEPAD and, 108
  political leadership in, 72–74
    (*See also* Nkrumah, Kwame)
  state socialism in, 72–73
Ghana empire, 30
Global warming, 25–26
Goats, 29
Gold, 84
Gold Coast, 31
Gold mining, 2, 10
Governance, economics and, 90–92
Government, 3
  colonial, 35–36

Grasslands, 22
Greater Somaliland, 37
Great Rift Valley, 3, 15–16
    lakes of, 16
Great Zimbabwe Ruins, 29

Hajj, 58
Harbors, 16
Harmattan, 20
Hausa-Fulani, 35, 37
Herbal practitioners, 87
Highlands, 23
Highways, 92–93
    colonial, 38
Historical geography, 28–40
    colonialism's impact in, 36–38
    colonial rule in, 35–36
    division of Africa in, 34–35
    early culture hearths in, 29–30
    European contact and slave trade
        in, 31–34
    independence struggles in, 38–40
    trade in, early West African, 30–31
History at a glance, 110–113
HIV/AIDS, 105
    in Botswana, 6, 94–95, 104, 105
    in Côte d'Ivoire, 99
    on life expectancy, 46
    in South Africa, 107
    in young, 94–95
Houphouët-Boigny, Félix, 71
Housing, urban, 49
Humidity, 21
Hunters, 25
Hunting and gathering, 29
    by Bushman, 104
Hutu-Tutsi conflict, 8–9, 102–103
Hydroelectricity, 17–18

Ibo, 37
Income per capita, 82, 83
Independence, 69–70
    economic development policies
        after, 75–76
    struggle for, 38–40

Indirect rule, colonial, 35–36
Infant mortality, 43, 46
Inflation, in Zimbabwe, 92
Informal sector, urban, 52–53
Information revolution, 94
Infrastructure, 92–94
    colonial, 38
Inheritance, dual, 64
Instability, political. See Political
    instability
International Monetary Fund (IMF), 77
    vs. Organization of African Unity,
        77–80
Internet, 93
Intertropical Convergence Zone, 20
Iron, 83–84
Islam, 58
    family size in, 45–46
    spread of, 29
Islamic law, 61
    in Nigeria, 99
Ivory Coast, 31

Jesus Christ, 58, 59–60
Jihad, 58
Jubba River, 7

Kabila, Joseph, 77
Kabila, Laurent, 72, 77
Kalahari Desert, 21, 104
Kampala, 48
Kano, 31
Kaunda, Kenneth, 72
Kel tagelmust, 62
Kente, 62
Kenya, 100, 101
    independence struggle in, 39–40
Kenyatta, Jomo, 40, 71
Kibaki, Mwai, 101
Kikuyu, 40
Koran, 58
Kush kingdom, 30

Lagos, 48, 49–52
Lagos Plan of Action, 78–79

Lake Chad, 7
Lake Msalawi, 16
Lakes, 16
Lake Tanganyika, 16
Lake Turkana, 16
Lake Victoria, 16
Land
    access to, 86–89
    in Africa, 7
    area of, 109
    features of, 14–16
Landscape, 2–3
Languages, 8, 55
Leaders for life, 71, 74
Lesotho, HIV/AIDS in, 95
Libation, for Onyame, 56–57
Liberia, child soldiers in, 96
Life and livelihood, 9
Life expectancy, 46–47
Lingua franca, 8
Livestock, 29, 89
Lualaba River, 17
Lumumba, Patrice, 75

Malaria, 21
Malawi, life expectancy and infant
    mortality in, 46
Mali, HIV/AIDS in, 95
Mali empire, 30
Mandela, Nelson, 6, 106
Manganese, 83–84
Maritime tropical air mass, 20
Marriage, 62–63, 66
Matatus, 53
Mau Mau conflicts, 40
Mecca, 58
Media, 93
Medicines, traditional, 87
Metals, precious, 10
Migration, rural-to-urban,
    48–54
    in Lagos, 49–52
    overurbanization from, 48
    transportation on, 53–54
    unemployment on, 49

urban housing on, 49
urban informal sector in, 52–53
Military coups, 11, 72, 74
    in Ghana, 73–74
Millet, 21
Mineral wealth, 83–86. *See also*
    specific minerals
    export of, 89–90
Minibuses (taxi), 53–54
    in Zimbabwe, 91–92
Missionaries, 34, 38, 59
Mobutu, Joseph, 75
Mobutu Sese Seko, 11, 72, 84
Moi, Daniel arap, 101, 108
Mortality, infant, 43, 46
Mosquitoes, disease-spreading, 21
Mountains, 15
Mount Kenya, 23
Mount Kilimanjaro, 15, 23
Mozambique
    independence in, 40
    life expectancy and infant mortality
        in, 46
Mugabe, Robert, 40, 74, 92
Muhammad, 58
Multinational corporations, 10–11
Multination state, 36–37
Multistate nation, 36, 37
Muslims. *See* Islam
Mzungu, 40

Names, 65–66
Namib, 21
Naming ceremonies, 65–66
National parks, 24
Nations, 36
    multistate, 36, 37
Nation-states, 36
Natural resources, 10, 82–86.
    *See also* specific resources
New Economic Partnership for
    Africa's Development (NEPAD),
    79–80, 108
Nigeria
    ethnic conflict in, 67

future of, 99–100
Ibos secession and Biafran War in, 75
oil in, 13, 83, 90, 99
political instability in, 37, 74
population of, 43
religious conflict in, 61
Niger River, 17
Nile River, 16–17
Nkrumah, Kwame, 38–39, 70, 72–74
Nok culture, 30
North Africa, 7
Nyerere, Julius, 72, 102

Obayifo, 57
Obonsam, 57
Ocean
on temperature variation, 20–21
Oil, 13, 82–83
in Angola, 83
export of, 90
in Gabon, 13, 103
in Nigeria, 13, 83, 90, 99
in Sudan, 13
Okada, 53
Okomfo, 56
Onyame, 56–57
Organization of African Unity (OAU), 70–71
vs. IMF and World Bank, 77–80
Orphans, AIDS, 64, 95
Overurbanization, 48

Paintings, rock, 29
Palm oil exports, 90
Palm trees, 24
Pan-African Highway, 93
Parks national, 24
Petroleum shortages, 91
Physical geography, 14–27
climate in, 18–21
desert in, 21
environmental problems in, 23–27
(See also Environmental problems)

highlands in, 23
land features in, 14–16
rivers in, 16–18
steppe in, 22–23
tropical rain forest in, 21–22
tropical savanna in, 22
Pilgrimage, Islamic, 58
Pineapple exports, 90
Plateau, 15
Poaching, 22, 25
Political allegiance, 64
Political borders, European drawing of, 35
Political history, 69–80
African Union in, 71
economic development policies in, 75–76
IMF/World Bank vs. OAU in, 77–80
independence in, 38–40, 69–70
Kwame Nkrumah and Ghana in, 72–74
leadership problems in, 71–72
Organization of African Unity in, 70–71, 77–80
political instability in, 76–77
post-independence chaos in, 74–75
Political instability
in Nigeria, 37, 74
reasons for, 76–77
Politics, 11
Polygamy, 63
Polytheism, 57
Population, 40–54, 109.
See also Settlement
concentration of, 43
density of, 41
dynamics of, 43–46
life expectancy and infant mortality on, 46–47
Wabenzi in, 47
Poultry, 90
Poverty, 9, 64, 82–86
urban, 82, 83
President for life, 71

Priest, in animism, 56
Primate cities, 48
Prosperity gospel, 59–61
Puntland, 101

Railroads, 92
Rainfall, in subsistence agriculture, 9, 86
Rain forest, tropical, 21–22
Ramadan, 58
Regions, 6
Religion, 56–61
    animism, traditional, 56–58
    Christianity, 58–59
    conflict and, 61
    Islam, 58
    prosperity gospel, 59–61
Religious conflict, 11
Resource curse, 10–11
Revolutionary United Front (RUF), 84–85
Rhino horn, 25
Rivers, 16–18. See also specific rivers
Roads, colonial, 38
Rock paintings, 29
Rural-to-urban migration, 48–54
Rush hour, 51–52
Rwanda, 102–103
    Hutu-Tutsi conflict in, 8–9

Safaris, 11, 22
Sahara Desert, 7, 21
    air mass from, 20
Sanctions, in animism, 58
Sankoh, Foday, 84–85
Satan, 57
Savanna, tropical, 22
Savanna grasslands, 3
Schools
    colonial introduction of, 38
    rural, 37
Science, 73
Secessionist movements, 74
Security, 12–13
Senegal, HIV/AIDS in, 95

Senegal River, 7
September 11, 2001, 12–13
Seraphim, 59
Serengeti National Park, 22
Settlement, 48–54. See also Population
    rural-to-urban migration in, 48–54
        (See also Migration)
    urbanization and primate cities in, 48
Severe acute respiratory syndrome (SARS), 12
Sharia, 61
    in Nigeria, 99
Sharing, 64
Sheep, 29
Sierra Leone
    child soldiers in, 96
    diamonds and conflict in, 84–85
    life expectancy and infant mortality in, 46
Silent trade, 31–32
Slavery, 4
    end of, 34
Slave trade, 32–34
Sleeping sickness, 21–22
Socialism, in Ghana, 72–73
Society. See Culture and society
Soldiers, child, 96–97
Somalia, 100, 101
Somaliland, 37, 101
Songhai empire, 30
Sorghum, 21
South Africa, 106–107
Southern Africa, 104–107
Soybean exports, 90
Spirits, 56
States, 36
    multination, 36–37
Steppe, 22–23
Structural Adjustment Program (SAP), 78–79
Subsistence agriculture, 9, 86–89
Sudan
    child soldiers in, 96
    ethnic conflict in, 66–67

land area of, 3
oil in, 13
Osama bin Laden in, 13
religious conflict in, 11
Swaziland, HIV/AIDS in, 95
Symbolism, 61–62

Tanzania, 100, 102
mountains of, 23
Taxi, minibus, 53–54, 91–92
Technology, 73
Tectonic activity, 16
Textiles, 62
Timber industry, 10
Timbuktu, 31
Tobacco, from Zimbabwe, 106
Tourism, 15
ecotourism, 22
safari, 11
Trade
in early West Africa, 30–31
silent, 31–32
slave, 32–34
Traditional medicines, 87
Traffic jams, 51–52
Transition zone, 16
Transportation, in cities, 53–54
Transportation network, 92–93
Triangular trade, 33
Tropical latitudes, 3–4
Tropical rain forest, 21–22
Tropical savanna, 22
Tro tro, 53
Tsetse fly, 21
Tuareg dress, 62
Tutsi, 8–9, 102–103

Uganda, 100
child soldiers in, 96
Unemployment, 49
Urban housing, 49
Urban informal sector, 52–53
Urbanization, 48

Vegetable exports, 90
Vegetation, 21–23
Victoria Falls, 17, 105
Volta River, 18

Wabenzi, 47
War. See also Conflict
child soldiers in, 96–97
Wealth
display of, 64
sharing of, 64
Weather
food security and, 27
rainfall in, 9, 86
West Africa, 4–6
early trade in, 30–31
future of, 99–100
Wildlife, 11
declining, 25
in tropical savanna, 22
Witches, 57
Wizards, 57
World Bank, 77
vs. Organization of African Unity,
77–80
Written records, 28

Yellow fever, 21
Yoruba, 37
Youth challenges, 94–97
HIV/AIDS in, 94–95
soldiers, 96–97

Zambezi River, 17
Zambia, life expectancy and infant
mortality in, 46
Zimbabwe, 105–106. See also
Mugabe, Robert
economy and governance in, 90–92
HIV/AIDS in, 95
independence in, 40
life expectancy and infant mortality
in, 46
Zionists, 59

All photographs are provided courtesy of Joseph R. Oppong.

Cover: Index Stock Imagery

JOSEPH R. OPPONG is Associate Professor of Geography at the University of North Texas (UNT) in Denton Texas, and a native of Ghana. He has about 16 years University teaching experience in Ghana, Canada, and the United States. Joseph has served as Chair of the Africa Specialty Group of the Association of American Geographers and is currently Chair of the Medical Geography Specialty Group. His research focuses on medical geography: the geography of disease and health care. Joseph has four children: Esther (co-author of *Ghana* and *Kenya* in the Modern World Nations Series), Daniel, Lydia, and Joseph David. Joseph enjoys research, photography, and teaching, especially taking university students on a life-transforming summer study abroad in Ghana.

CHARLES F. ("FRITZ") GRITZNER is Distinguished Professor of Geography at South Dakota University in Brookings. He is now in his fifth decade of college teaching and research. During his career, he has taught more than 60 different courses, spanning the fields of physical, cultural, and regional geography. In addition to his teaching, he enjoys writing, working with teachers, and sharing his love for geography with students. As consulting editor for the MODERN WORLD NATIONS series, he has a wonderful opportunity to combine each of these "hobbies." Fritz has served as both President and Executive Director of the National Council for Geographic Education and has received the Council's highest honor, the George J. Miller Award for Distinguished Service. In March 2004, he won the Distinguished Teaching award from the American Association of Geographers at their annual meeting held in Philadelphia.